LET GO AND Live

JAMES DYCHE

WESTBOW
PRESS®
A DIVISION OF THOMAS NELSON
& ZONDERVAN

Scripture taken from the King James Version of the Bible.

"Scripture quotations are from the ESV® Bible (The Holy Bible, English Standard Version®), copyright © 2001 by Crossway, a publishing ministry of Good News Publishers. Used by permission. All rights reserved."

This book is a work of non-fiction. Unless otherwise noted, the author and the publisher make no explicit guarantees as to the accuracy of the information contained in this book and in some cases, names of people and places have been altered to protect their privacy.

WestBow Press books may be ordered through booksellers or by contacting:

WestBow Press
A Division of Thomas Nelson & Zondervan
1663 Liberty Drive
Bloomington, IN 47403
www.westbowpress.com
1 (866) 928-1240

ISBN: 978-1-9736-0017-6 (sc)
ISBN: 978-1-9736-0016-9 (hc)
ISBN: 978-1-9736-0018-3 (e)

Library of Congress Control Number: 2017913280

Print information available on the last page.

WestBow Press rev. date: 9/22/2017

I dedicate this book to our heavenly Father. I give a special thanks to my dad, James, and my mother-in-law, Sharon. Without the precious memories that we shared together, all of this would not be possible. A special thanks to Lori Haislip, Odessa Criales-Smith, Ruth Minnick, Jeanne Martin and many others for their endless prayers. And to my wife, Jenny, my beautiful rose, I love you!

For mom, the strongest woman I know.

CONTENTS

CHAPTER ONE

What is Life?

And this is eternal life, that they may know you the only true God, and Jesus Christ whom you have sent.

—*John 17:3*

W hat is life?

This is a question that has been pondered for many centuries by many great people from all walks and beliefs. The answer is always different and usually unique in its interpretation. This is not a question for a few or a chosen people; rather, it is an everyday question for everyday people.

Life is ever before us, and the answer that we give defines the very being that is within us. We are on a test track for eternity—a proving ground for the words we believe, speak, and act upon. The answer to life lies deep and hidden in the fabric of our being, just waiting to be revealed. When the layers of life are peeled back and the veil is removed, we have a clearer image of a new creature in a new creation—a creature transformed in a view of a creator. It is a perfect opportunity of heaven interchanging with earth in the personal work of a Holy God and his Son, Jesus.

> And they have conquered him by the blood of the
> Lamb and by the word of their testimony, for they
> loved not their lives even unto death. (Revelation
> 12:11)

I want to share this very personal part of my life because I truly believe there is power in his testimony that he surely shares with the people he loves. It was in letting go that I obtained life, and it was in the power of his testimony that I was able to begin to have victories. You may ask yourself what would qualify you for such a gift. Only believe!

> But overhearing what they said, Jesus said to the
> ruler of the synagogue official, "Do not fear, only
> believe." (Mark 5:36)

My story started in what seemed like the deepest recess of darkness that I could care to remember. I was only sixteen years old the first time I knew God was pulling on my heart. I yearned for freedom, as most teenagers do, but I had no concept of what freedom actually meant. Freedom at that time was getting out on my own away from the structure of my family, and it came at a great sacrifice. The price of freedom isn't cheap, and it usually accompanies a degree from the school of hard knocks. Little did I know that Christ was my freedom from my perception of life.

> For freedom Christ has set us free. Stand firm
> therefore, and do not submit again to the yoke of
> slavery. (Galatians 5:1)

At times, our lives play out a lot differently than we perceive they will or should. We look at a carnal means to survive and to be successful, but life presents itself as so much more. We gauge success by what we accomplish in life, and we fulfill our lives through the experience of it. Our perception of life is truly rocked when life itself enters the scene. When God reveals himself to us, it is a monumental moment because everything is about to change. I dismissed his calls at the time, but God never left. He remained right by my side, even though I didn't desire him.

Thoughts are unspoken words that have yet to be birthed by the power of the tongue. Thoughts often turn into words that shape and mold what we perceive and believe. Many decisions start with thoughts and then with words. I was beginning to value the choice of my thoughts and words. They are more powerful than we could ever imagine. I couldn't wait to leave home, and I got my wish.

I left home to join the military, and I was going to serve in my first deployment overseas. Before my departure, my dad shared with me his wisdom and passion for life, which was family and living for them. He was devoted and faithful to us. He gave his life for us and was always a man of his word. Integrity and truth were vital parts to having a relationship with him. At the time I couldn't even be truthful with myself, so I left with few words.

My mom was different. She was nurturing and caring, and even when we were wrong, she would find a way to communicate with us through love. She was a virtuous woman who cared little for herself. Just like my dad, she gave her life for the family. Patience and kindness ran deep in her heart, and forgiveness was a staple in any relationship. Love was her language.

When I was overseas, I lived a very riotous life. I was a product of my own words. Growing up, we have to make difficult decisions that forge life as we know it. When I wasn't overseas, I resided in the part of Northern California that is known as the Bay Area. It was a long way from West Virginia, where I was raised. When we become consumed with the wrong perception of life, we lose track of what really matters. Although I didn't tell them at the time, I missed my family dearly. I would cling to the phone calls I received from home. They meant everything.

One afternoon as I was going about my business, I received the most dreaded phone call of my life. My dad had been diagnosed with a very aggressive lung cancer. At the age of forty, he was given a short time to live if immediate action wasn't taken. My heart dropped from my chest. I felt broken and completely undone at the uncertainty of the unknown. It was a place that none of us wanted to walk, but we were about to do so nevertheless. There was one thing that I was certain of—I needed help, and I needed it immediately. My help had been with me all along, but I had chosen to be blinded to that truth.

> So we can confidently say, "The Lord is my helper. I will not fear. What can man do to me?" (Hebrews 13:6)

When there is no knowledge of God's love, fear is ever present even at the first sign of trouble. At the time, I had traveled only by plane from coast to coast, but this time I was driving. I packed my bags and headed east into the uncertainty of the unknown. The drive from California to West Virginia felt as if it lasted for an eternity. I had a lot of time to think about my life. We get to know our real selves when we pack all our possessions in a car and holler, "Road trip!" It seems as if we can become completely lost.

Life certainly happens whether we are ready or not. Most things are hidden from our understanding until we experience and have a go-around with them. Over the few years I was in the service, I crossed many miles of oceans without knowing the depths of them. At least when we had fire drills, one of the officers would yell, "Closest land is seventeen hundred feet, so let's get this fire out!" Sometimes things aren't as visible as we would like them to be, but we have to move forward.

> Therefore, since we are surrounded by so great a cloud of witnesses, let us also lay aside every

weight, and sin which clings so closely, and let us
run with endurance the race that is set before us.
(Hebrews 12:1)

To be honest, the race I was running was a race of destruction,
and it was leaving a path of lies in its wake. Alcoholism, drug
addiction, and divorce were far from my thoughts, but my heart
was speaking loudly as my lips would oppose anyone who wanted
to help. Our words always have a way of revealing the true nature
of our hearts. I had plenty of time in that car to convince myself
that I was tough and that I would be able to hide my true feelings
from my dad. Boy, was I wrong.

Most always, a kind word and a demonstration of love is all
we need. This can help to break up the hard ground of our hearts
and prepare them for seed. What I am most thankful for is my
family, which God placed me with. I remember opening the front
door of my home, and there was my family to greet me with kind
words and open arms of love to relieve me.

Gracious words are like a honeycomb, sweetness
to the soul and health to the body. (Proverbs 16:24)

Walking through that door and looking to the right, I saw
my dad sitting in the recliner. He had just made it home from a
twenty-seven-day stay in the hospital. He looked at me and began
to smile. He wrapped his arms around me and told me, "I love
you." I could feel the warmth of his embrace as I was saturated
with love from him and my family members. It's hard to resist
when someone loves you with all his or her heart. It's something
you feel at first, but then you begin to *know* it. People can give
parts of themselves to us regardless of the situation. It's in this
that we see a glimpse of heaven. It is in those small and precious
moments that we see the image of a living and loving Father and
become one under that banner of love.

Over the next few months, we watched Dad begin to go into remission, and the healing process began. He'd lost three-quarters of his lung, he had a 50 percent chance between life and death, and he was back with us. The great news was that we could return to normal and get a fresh start on life. It was nice to have him back any way we could get him.

Near-death experiences usually bring focus back to the family and offer a new vigor for life. They can also bring back a fervency to know God from the perspective of greater wisdom. My dad would chat with me about God and his Son, Jesus, and my dad would share his experience of lying on the recovery table and hearing God calling him. I remember vividly his descriptions of Jesus and how my dad asked for mercy. He cried aloud for help for his family! He was able to look down on his own body. He said, "It looked cold and lifeless."

He asked God, "Can I get my family ready?

After that he was granted his petition, he said, and his spirit gently floated down like a feather and returned, bringing life and warmth to his being. I stood looking at him in awe. Something within me identified with the truth he was speaking to me. It gripped my heart and captivated me because my dad was a truthful man. I had never known him to lie, so I just believed him, but I had a hard time wrapping my head around his story.

When I was younger, my solution to a problem was to run. When it comes to a son, a father's love means everything, but what I didn't realize was that a father's love is even greater for his son. There is no amount of distance that love cannot travel. It's far beyond our wildest imaginations and dreams. Nothing can break that bond of love.

> No, in all these things we are more than conquerors through him who loved us. For I am sure that neither death nor life, nor angels nor rulers, nor things present nor things to come, nor powers, nor

height nor depth, nor anything else in all creation
will be able to separate us from the love of God in
Christ Jesus our Lord. (Romans 8:37–38)

Over the years it has dawned on me that God used my family
mightily to show me what unconditional love really is. It's a
wonderful day when we come to that realization. God purposed
many men and women to be bold and act out upon faith to access
grace. His grace is the unmerited and unearned favor of God.
Stepping out into the unknown takes faith and belief in the unseen.
God acted through each of them as they let go and believed!

Love is patient and kind; Love does not envy and
boast; it is not arrogant or rude. It does not insist
on its own way; it is not irritable or resentful, it
does not rejoice at wrong doing, but rejoices with
the truth. Love bears all things, believes all things,
hopes all things, endure all things. Love never
ends. (1 Corinthians 13:4–8)

A year or so later we received the news that my dad's cancer
had returned. This was a true hit to the heart. The disease was
traveling through his blood stream and spreading fast. We
were told to make the necessary preparations for him. My dad's
response to the news was love. I'm sure he was overwhelmed, but
he reached out for all of us. He was one of the bravest men I have
ever known.

Some of the sweetest words that can be exchanged are the
blessings of people you love when they are trying to tell you how
they really feel as they lie dying in their bodies. Without a shadow
of a doubt, I know my dad truly loved. My response when I got
the news of his cancer was to run, but his love and faith cried out
loud and clear. He patiently awaited my presence, and he had kind
words for me. His best interest was on our behalf, and his hands

were open to forgiveness. He bore his heart toward us, believing, hoping, and enduring until the end. One word that never failed him was *love*.

My mom spent day and night with him. It was as if her world had stopped. She was a mother hen by nature and shielded us from a lot of pain under the cover of her wings. My brothers and I all needed Mom, and even in her suffering she comforted. I really share all this because we just don't wake up one day and find ourselves a certain person. This is something that we learn, and it usually comes from the inside and manifests outward. That's the importance of love. Even in the worse circumstances it never fails.

> Fight the good fight of faith. Take hold of the eternal life to which you were called and about which you made the good confession in the presence of many witnesses. (1 Timothy 6:12)

After a few weeks in the hospital, my dad was tired and in pain. When we fight we can get awfully weary, and our spirits can get low. My dad had made his good confession of God and his faith toward Jesus in front of many and was taking hold of eternal life. He expressed his deepest love to my mother and told her he was ready to go home. At that time, none of us understood what that entailed. He described how heaven opened and he heard, "It is time." Sometimes we just can't fathom that in the moment.

Later that week he passed in the middle of the night. We all had an expectation of hope that he would beat the cancer. I truly believe that he did, but never the way we pictured it. The immediate pattern of thought is that the person you love is now gone, but the eternal blueprint of God is life and it will be forever and ever. It was a seed God planted in me even when I looked at Dad and tried not to "lose it." Even as I resisted in my pain, God never relented. His love wrapped around me despite my immediate shock and grief.

The next few days were very rough. As many do, I found

myself searching every crevice for just a crumb of peace. It's odd the things I remembered at that time—conversations and glimpses of Dad all the way back to childhood. It was truly a roller coaster of emotion. His passing brought my heart to a very tender spot. This sort of event is a critical time for the heart also because we are confronted with the choice of accepting the truth or denying it. One of the hardest things I had to do was accept this truth: he was not gone; rather, he now has life in God through Jesus. Although it was one of the hardest truths for me to understand, it has been the one I have held closest to my heart.

> I have stored up your *word* in my heart, That I might
> not sin against you. (Psalm 119:11; emphasis added)

I have learned that we hold on to words that have the power to bind or free us. It is a common saying that time heals all wounds, but I have found this not to be completely true. Time only diminishes the pain because we learn to adapt and move on. My dad, over the years, had stored up God's Word in his heart. As little as it seems, the impact of one meaningful word can cause new life to come about. We can never underestimate small beginnings because it's through the small things that we learn about larger things. It's in larger things we learn the infinite possibilities of God's eternal Word. His Word never changes, but it does change everything around it.

Dad's legacy was successful and honored by God. Dad had honored us with his word and had done the very best he could do to get his family together. In return, God gave my dad eternal life regardless of his circumstances and the promise of his family.

> For by grace you have been saved through faith.
> And this is not of your own doing; it is a gift of
> God, not a result of works, so that no one may
> boast. (Ephesians 2:8–9)

> Now faith is the assurance of things hoped for,
> the conviction of things not seen. (Hebrews 11:1)

Waking up on the day of the funeral was the hardest thing I ever had to do in my life. The thing I remember most is having a conviction in my heart that I needed God. I thought the pain would go away if, for one second, I could know that he was with me. I went to the car to grab the crucifix that was hanging from the mirror. As I was putting it on, it fell apart, and the only thing that was left was the cross in my right hand. It was God's way of saying, "I am with you."

I could only believe what Dad witnessed to us because it was the only thing that brought peace. It all came crashing down quickly when the brevity of this life sunk in. Looking down on my dad as he lay in the coffin suddenly brought floods of emotions I couldn't control. Being honest, I was very confused and angry with God and simply didn't understand. I felt robbed as Dad's death seared my conscience.

Still, God was my help and my comfort. So many of my dad's family members and friends reached out with warm gestures and nice stories. Psalm 23 was scripted on the memoriam. As the pastor was reading the eulogy, he blessed my dad and so many others with his kind words and actions.

> The Lord is my shepherd; I shall not want. He makes me lie down in green pastures. He leads me beside still waters. He restores my soul. He leads me in paths of righteousness for his name's sake. Even though I walk through the valley of the shadow of death I will fear no evil, for you are with me; your rod and your staff, they comfort me. You prepare a table before me in the presence of my enemies; you anoint my head with oil; my cup overflows. Surely goodness and mercy shall

follow me all the days of my life, and I shall dwell
in the house of the Lord forever. (Psalm 23:1–6)

It took years for me to digest what he was saying that day. In the moment, a few words would have sufficed—just to be able to tell Dad "I love you" or just to hear "I'll see you later" back from him.

We have to let go of those last words that you "could have spoken." Being thankful for the time you have and not holding on to your true feelings for people—that is what truly matters. The problem is that we are not guaranteed tomorrow, so we must release our words and hearts to the ones we love and let the rest of the chips lie as they fall.

There was a very young family several doors down from my dad's hospital room. The husband and wife were in their early twenties and had two beautiful children. The young man had the same cancer that Dad had. Visiting Dad as many times as I did, I met and talked with this family. The young man died a few weeks after I met him, and I thought to myself that we had met in order to learn a lesson on thankfulness. The other lesson I learned was that cancer—or any disease—is inhumane because it diminishes the hope and dreams of so many families, and that made me sad.

After knowing how the cancer ravaged my dad's body, I found it difficult to believe in my heart that Dad had any peace or comfort. It was hard to imagine that he was one of God's sheep lying in green pastures and beside still waters. After we had laid him to rest, many people came to comfort us, but truthfully I just wanted to be by myself. I just wanted Dad back. At the time, I couldn't see an inch before my face, but the truth still remained and was very much alive.

Anyone who does not love does not know God,
because God is love. (1 John 4:8)

Learning how to love out of a void of hurt and total darkness is hard to do. Each and every person has the ability to love and can choose to love. To know that you are loved regardless of actions is wrenching to the heart. No matter how far you run, God's arms are open and waiting. Even when we are at the end of our rope, we tend to hold on when all that has to happen is to let go.

I always wondered how my dad loved me the way he did, but I understand now that love is not only an action but the greatest gift of all. To believe God is love frees us from anything we are willing to surrender to.

There are times when we are prodigal and ask for our portion, and we take it into the world and waste it on what we believe is right.

There are times when we have a loss for words, and there is a famine in the land. In my grief, words seemed to be trodden under foot and they fell short of the way I meant for them to sound. I experienced this as I stood by my dad's coffin wanting to say all the right things, but the only thing that was coming out was all wrong. There were so many people, but being there by the graveside was like being in a cold and distant place. In those final moments, closure bore down and the realization came that the one I loved had just passed.

The moments we share with each other are so important and real. We dismiss the moments we have in life because, at the time, they seem trivial and don't seem to matter. That is a great tragedy and one of the misconceptions we have about life. The knowledge of God and his Son brings life and love. The moments that we share are ordained by one who is greater than anything. When we have these moments, it is as if his life plays a part in ours, and as we yield to it, the picture of a dad loving a wayward son is so real. It becomes part of us and begins to live, move, and materialize. We truly are his offspring.

Although the pain of that day was almost more than I could bear at the time, something began to dwell from within that was a reminder that there is an abundance of life that we haven't seen yet. It has been sixteen years since that day. The way I feel and view it all now is totally different. One thing has remained throughout all these years, however, and that is the constant flow of love I have known that heals and restores from the inside out. This kind of love brings us from creature into the view of a creator. That kind of love enables us to let go and grab onto something greater. It enables us to embrace life and love ourselves with no regard or reserve.

———◆———

As a good friend of mine would say,
that is "to live life out loud!"

CHAPTER TWO

$$\text{Framed by Faith}$$

> By faith we understand that the universe was
> created by the word of God, so that what is seen
> was not made out of things that are visible.
>
> —*Hebrews 11:3*

F aith is having confidence in another's testimony. It is the
substance of things hoped for, the evidence of things not
seen. It is truly a gift from God that comes out of the hearts of
all people. Faith enables us to know God and his Son, Jesus. It is
an empowerment that allows us to see the work of God. He has
allotted each of us a measure of faith, but we must choose to use
it and believe upon it.

The intent of the scriptures is clear and very powerful. Jesus
performed many miracles in the presence of his disciples, and
many of these were not recorded. Most would ask, "Why would
he do that?"

The best answer that any man could give would be faith.
Oftentimes we are in a reflective period in which we are trying
to find the purpose that we serve. It can be a very hectic time as
trial after trial tests the fabric of our being. This is the time when
we often look over our lives for the right words to say. It can also

be an opportunity to hope for the evidence of things not seen and be an agent of change by gazing in the mirror of God's Word and speaking it out into the realm of faith. God's Word has the ability to change even the smallest of circumstances, altering the course of defeat to victory.

The question that I have asked of God most is, "Why must I seek you?"

It is strange to say, but after all the running, I have found that God was never far from me even when I didn't choose him. It took seven years after my dad died, but after a few heartfelt words as I knelt before God, he was never closer.

The word *genesis* means the "origin" or "root." It is the beginning or start of something. This is very significant because most of us begin in a place without form—a void full of darkness just like the earth. But then God speaks. At the sound of his voice, creation begins to spring up, and life comes forth. The sound and warmth of his voice is the framework and entrance of life and the beginning of our very existence. It is his living Word. His Word and breath of life usher his presence and all that he is to those who need more of it.

> This is he who came by water and blood—Jesus Christ; not by the water only but by the water and the blood. And the Spirit is the one who testifies, because the Spirit is the truth. [7] For there are three that testify: the Spirit and the water and the blood; and these three agree. If we receive the testimony of men, the testimony of God is greater, for this is the testimony of God that he has borne
>
> concerning his Son. (1 John 5: 6–9)

Jesus said, "I am the Alpha and the Omega, the first and the last, the beginning and the end." (Revelation 22:13).

15

In the beginning we see God as the creator of heaven and earth. The Spirit of God moved upon the face of the waters and then God spoke his Word. There is an establishment from the very beginning that bears record in heaven and cries aloud to the darkness. It shakes the very foundations of the ways of the world. It speaks: "And God said!"

Seeing the creative nature of God is just the beginning. As God spoke, things just came into being. Knowing that his Word starts merely as a seed and then becomes fruit is a beginning of good things. He is the giver of every perfect gift from above but we must understand that his Word is the bridge that connects the gap between heaven and earth. We see in the beginning all three bearing record to the earth. God was speaking; his Word was performing and demonstrating, and his spirit hovered over. Heaven and earth were in alignment with one another. It seems at times that these three are separate, but they always work as one.

> In the beginning was the Word, and the Word was with God, and the Word was God. He was in the beginning with God. All things were made through him, and without him was not anything made that was made. In him was life, and the life was the light of men. (John 1:1–4)

We have the choice to present the gospel as an ancient book full of knowledgeable words or as the way to reveal the Father and his fullness. According to the scriptures, we see that the Word was there in the beginning. The Word is defined as "logos." It is a title of Christ emphasizing his own deity of who God is and what he is like. We see that the Word was with God and was God. The nature of the Word is to reveal the Father and his fullness. Without the Word, there would be no way to the Father. It is his bridge from heaven to earth.

From the very beginning, God's creative nature was through

the Word. It was, is, and always will be the way God uses to reach creation. The Word is the seed from heaven and is God's reflection and nature to the earth. It is an amazing fact that, naturally, a seed needs dirt to support and nourish it, and it needs moisture to begin to grow. When God created man, he breathed into his nostrils and created him from the dust. He breathed the breath of life, and man became living, breathing. And then God moved upon man.

Breath is the first exchange we see between God and man. This breath of life is vital to understanding the blueprint because it's in his breath that he brings forth life. Only by faith can we see God forming man from dust to life. It is in this exchange that it is possible to believe that we are his offspring. Without this breath we would never exist to have light and life. It is the foundation of the creative. He breathes! We receive!

> The Spirit of God has made me, and the breath of
> the Almighty gives me life. (Job 33:4)

We are created in the image of God. It is within his breath that the Word forms man and springs forth light. When the Word is released, the spirit goes forth to create and renew the face of the ground. It's in this breath that there is a holy connection between the Father and his children. We are blessed to know that we are his, and we are birthed by the command of his breath. His Word is the thread that binds two hearts as one while the spirit of the Lord blows upon it. His Word is like a mirror. It reflects ancient truths through us in the present.

> And the Word became flesh and dwelt among us,
> and we have seen the glory, glory as of the only Son
> from the Father, full of grace and truth. (John 1:14)

The word *glory* here in the scriptures is descriptive of an awesome light that radiates from God's presence and is associated with him and all that he is. We experience this as the illumination that happens when the spirit is in complete darkness. We can see through creation that man was just dirt until God breathed into him and formed him. The Word became flesh and dwelt among us. Most believe this to be the incarnation of the Son of God. The incarnation of God goes far beyond a biblical story of Jesus being sent, but it is his living Word that takes abode in our darkest places and springs forth as glorious light. Jesus is that living Word.

God's Word is the foundation and the seed that brings forth life and is the light of men. I truly believe that God is not looking for a temple or a building made with hands; rather, his dwelling place is with humankind. The illumination is his Word in our inward parts. While we are in the midst of darkness, we find that our spirit searches for the inward truth in any situation, but the truth of the matter is that he searches for us in darkness and desires to illuminate the body, soul, and spirit with the revelation and understanding of him.

Creation responded as the voice of the Lord resounded, ringing out into all that wasn't. Its only response was to spring forth from the dirt and just be. I could imagine that his voice was thunderous and filled everything as life exploded from his breath and lips. We have to feel the same way, as we are earthen vessels waiting upon the warmth of his breath and the invitation of his Word. In the beginning, God simply spoke. That's pure and simple.

> He sent his word and healed them, and delivered
> them from their destruction. (Psalm 107:20)

From the very first time I heard his voice, my heart was moved. Even though I didn't want to listen, my heart responded. The unseen miracles that happened in the days when I first heard his voice until the day of surrendering were countless. The miraculous happens when a hardened heart becomes fertile ground for God's Word. For humankind, the time we go without seems to be an eternity, but in the eyes of God it's just a moment. We act as though the moments don't matter, but they truly do.

The Word of God is infallible, and his truth witnesses to the people. He sends his Word forth to heal and deliver humankind. His scriptures are forever; they are binding and full of authority. His Word is near always. It is in the mouth and the hearts of everyone who has breath. His Word was sent because of this very reason. It is impossible for God to lie. This is where we see the world being framed by the Word of God. The world cries out for circumstances and trials, but the Word of God demands truth.

Another purpose of the Word of God is to build faith. Faith is the substance of things hoped for. The result is that the things we hoped for become tangible. This is when we realize that he is so close and that his Word is heartfelt and full of gratitude. His Word is lovely, loyal, and trustful. It strengthens us with the attitude to grow and to hope.

His Word was not only sent to fulfill our hope and bring substance; it was also a gift that would enable us to know him and move in him. His Word bears witness with us as it fills the gap of heaven and earth. The Word searches the heart until it gets to the root or the beginning of it. The one thing I have found through all this is that the secret to a merry heart is to surrender everything to God.

> And the angel answered him, "I am Gabriel. I stand in the presence of God, and I was sent to speak to you and to bring you the good news. And behold you will be silent and unable to speak until the day that these things take place, because you did not believe my words, which will be fulfilled in their time." (Luke 1:19–20)

It is the unbelief of humankind that shuts up faith. In the gospel of Luke, Zechariah was silenced and unable to speak until he believed. God's plan still went forth regardless. The Word persevered, causing faith to come forth even from the dimmest places. Zechariah's wife, Elizabeth, was barren, and they were both up there in age. The angel Gabriel delivered the good news that she would give birth to a son named John who would prepare the people for the Lord. At this point they had two choices: they could believe what God spoke or not. What we fail to see is that God's Word always fulfills what it has to fulfill. God's Word is not dependent upon humankind; instead, humankind is dependent on the Word. During this time, the hearts of Zechariah and Elizabeth were being prepared for more than a son named John. Their hearts were being prepared for a savior.

> Your word is a lamp to my feet and a light to my path. (Psalm 119:105)

During the time of preparation there are a lot of unanswered questions. It is a time during which things seem hidden and unknown. The Word of God is a lamp stand and a great source of knowledge and understanding. His Holy Spirit is a guide into the deeper places of God, awakening the human spirit to the call of his light. For Zechariah this was a time of silence before God, and for Elizabeth it was a five-month period of being hidden. The preparation time is critical because it reveals the true nature of the heart.

After Elizabeth conceived, she kept herself hidden for five months. The number five represents grace throughout the scriptures. During this time, we see the witness of Elizabeth.

She declares, "Thus the Lord has done for me in the days he looked on me, to take away my reproach among people." (Luke 1:25)

The word *reproach* means to heap insults or find fault. It is a state of disgrace. While reproach does happen, grace and truth correspond with the living reality of God's Word. The picture that we see being painted is a barren woman and her faith that comes in accord and agreement with the Word. The invisible and unseen are birthed by the power of covenant.

The fullness of God's grace and truth is not only one of his attributes, it also comes in his person and the personal work of God. The Word of God is the power and fullness of his covenant. The word *covenant* means an agreement between two parties. It is a legal document by which property is transferred to heirs, usually upon death. There are three who witness in heaven, and they are the Father, the Word, and the Spirit. Father is the heir of all things, the Word is his will and testament, and the Spirit is the truth that bears witness.

The beautiful part is this all connects with humankind so that we can see the purpose of his Word working through his creation. He chose to work through many individuals in order to bring forth the fullness of himself. This is one way we see the king and his kingdom. We see it through the shadows and types. We see this from the very beginning all the way to the end. The Word is truth and full of grace to those who seek after it. It unlocks the secret things and causes them to come forth from mystery to reality.

———◆———

The knowledge of the Father and his Word is for those who remain hidden in him, underneath the shadow of his wings. The reproach is taken away at this time. In these periods of life we see the insults and the disgraces fade away and become pale to God's Word. In turning to God and trusting him, we let go of all the things that hold us back from meaningful covenant. The power of his covenant comes to those who know this secret. The secret is that the way up is down.

CHAPTER THREE

From Shadow to Light

T he first chapter of the gospel of Luke is great imagery of the shadowed treasures coming to light. Zechariah was in the eighth course of priesthood by the division of Abijah. His name meant that God had remembered while his course meant that God was his Father. It is evident that what God has remembered is his covenant with his people. What is less evident is that God desires to be a Father to the fatherless. He desires to share his life with ours in the capacity of his fullness.

Zechariah has a wife named Elizabeth, who was from the lineage of Aaron. Her name meant "God's promise" or "oath of God" while her lineage was defined as a "high mountain." She was to give birth to a son, and his name was to be John, which means "God is gracious." God wanted humankind to know that he had not forgotten his people. Sometimes it seems as if we are forgotten, but God's promise and affirmation of his truth are our bond for eternity. In their family, none was called John. There are so many times we can see God's grace in the Old Testament through the shadows, but we see here that the forerunner is not only John; rather, it is the grace of God. It signifies at this time that the people had never seen grace like this before.

We also see a transition getting ready to happen before John is even out of Elizabeth's womb. The angel Gabriel declares, "And he will turn many of the children of Israel to the Lord their God, and he will go in the spirit of Elijah, to turn the hearts of the fathers to the children and the disobedient to the wisdom of the just, to make ready for the Lord a people prepared" (Luke 1:16–17).

The Word will always point back to God. The name Elijah means "Yahweh is God." In basic and simple terms, his name simply means "he is." To go in the spirit of Elijah would be to go in his Holy Spirit as "he is." The Word is a perfect reflection of God himself. It is not only what he sent, but it is God. A vessel that turns to God can be filled. The only way we can be prepared is to be made ready with his Word.

And the angel said to her:

> Do not be afraid, Mary, for you have found favor with God. And behold, you will conceive in your womb and bear a son, and you shall call his name Jesus. He will be great and will be called the Son of the Most High. And the Lord God will give to him the throne of his father David, and he will reign over the house of Jacob forever, and of his kingdom there will be no end. (Luke 1:30–33)

The angel Gabriel was sent to Mary with the favor of God. Again, this favor translates as grace. In this story we see all three bearing witness in the earth. This story can be equated as new life and birth, but it is important that we see that this is where God sent his Word. Gabriel visited in the sixth month signifying the number of man. This is where we truly capture the essence of God's Word because it becomes flesh not only witnessing in the heaven but also in the earth realm. He is truly God, and truly man being born from above and also being born by flesh overshadowed by the Holy Spirit.

> And Mary said to the angel, "How will this be, since I am a virgin?"

> And the angel answered her, "The Holy Spirit will come upon you, and the power of the Most High will overshadow you. Therefore the child to be born, will be called holy, The Son of God." (Luke 1:34–35)

A short while later Mary said, "Behold I am the servant of the Lord; let it be according to your word."

The words that were spoken became a covenant between God and his servant Mary as he enveloped her in the cloud. Mary consented after God had placed his seed and desires in her heart. God came upon Mary and then breathed his Word, setting forth the shadows of the dwelling place of God. It is in his creation that God sets forth a time of intimacy during which the Word becomes flesh for the power and glory of God.

It's hard to believe that God would choose to allow us to be temples that he can overshadow, but it is a very present truth. God is love. His Word embodies us, and his nature begins to take root. He prepares a place for us! His breath stokes the embers of our passion consuming all that we are so that we can be more like him. His passion for us is like a consuming fire that keeps the temple lit. It consumes all that is not God. In the Old Testament we read that the requirement for the temple is that the fire on the altar must burn constantly. This is not only achieved by faith, it is also his passion for us that allows the temple to be full of light. He is that fire!

I believe Mary's faith heralded the heavens and earth as her womb was filled with the fullness of God himself. Intimacy with God cannot be described as humankind would describe intimacy in a realm of the five senses; rather, it seeks out after everything that is holy and separated to God. This intimacy is consensual. The scriptures show that Mary opened and bore her heart before

God. This kind of intimacy is given only by God and received by humankind. That's why God is love—because he gave himself!

The time of preparation and covering is a time to listen, hear, and receive the engrafted Word of God that changes us. We have to know the time of our visitation because shortly thereafter we experience habitation. At his visitation we receive the vital Word that is needed for habitation. His Word is consistent, not persistent as it flows from heaven to earth. It is under the shadow that we see the birth of this new life. This time is not to be rushed or pushed through; rather, we have to use this time of favor to embrace the truth of his Word.

> So that they even carried out the sick into the streets and laid them on cots and mats; that as Peter came by at least his shadow might fall on some of them. (Acts 5:15)

This overshadowing just didn't happen once; it was a pattern into the most holy and sacred place. It is under this shadow of the Almighty that we see the possibilities of habitation. We think of a shadow as a form of darkness, but his shadow is a place of refuge and protection. The thing that rings true is that we don't have to look far to see his Word at work. The Word embodies the hearts and souls of humankind. It becomes!

It wasn't the shadow of Peter that was falling upon them; it was the Holy Spirit witnessing the Word at work. Peter was releasing what was in him. Just a few chapters back we see him denying the Lord, but in one gracious act of Word, Peter was moving with compassion and fervor.

Jesus simply said to Peter, "Feed my sheep" (John 21:17).

> Jesus answered him, "If anyone loves me, he will keep my word, and my Father will love him, and we will come to him and make our home with him." (John 14:23)

The time had come, and Elizabeth bore her son. The circumcision of the child was to happen on the eighth day. There were many family members who would have been happy if his name was Zechariah after his father, but God had other plans.

Elizabeth answered, "His name is John." (Luke 1:60).

Immediately people began to ask questions about his name. Then Zechariah released his faith by writing "John" on the writing tablet. His mouth was opened and his tongue loosed and he spoke. His silence was over as soon as he released his faith. Soon after Zechariah was filled with the Holy Spirit and began to prophesy, calling forth the holy covenant and the oath of graciousness that God remembered.

John would go on to announce the firstborn of many sons. He was truly a prophet, and his voice announced the call of the true Lamb of God. He would make known the knowledge of salvation to his people and lead them to the one who would forgive them of all sin. He would make ready a people for the light of God and the key to sonship. His message was a call to the remembrance of God's tender mercy and righteousness, not only to his people but also to generation after generation forever and ever. He was a sunrise that shall visit us from on high to set light into the darkened places of our hearts.

God's Word guides us into the way of peace. When we have peace, we learn to trust God and move away from the impossibilities of humankind into the possible with God. At first Zechariah and Elizabeth didn't have it all figured out, but their hearts were before God. It's faith that opens the door to the impossible, and it's grace that enables us to see God's power and abilities at work through his Word. Through him all things are brought from darkness into the light.

> So faith comes from hearing, and hearing through
> the word of Christ. (Romans 10:17)

The angel Gabriel stood in the presence of God but also ushered the heavenly message to both Elizabeth and Mary of the new birth they would both experience. God is a sovereign God. His Word is a surety and never changes, but it also has to do with our response to him. It is in the response that he tries the heart and pulls on the reins. His Word seeks us out until it gets to the root of the matter. The Word is our avenue for change.

It is not only about God seeking us; it is also about our required response that changes the heart and produces the fruit of his Word. Zechariah and Elizabeth were both righteous before God but had a hard time believing. I could imagine that, for those five months, the mercy of God as he washed over Elizabeth for the reproach among the people. Zechariah simply did not believe the Word, but God was patient. I truly believe it is not the ability of the heart; rather, it is the God-given desire that allows us to receive his Word. We exchange our lives for His.

> And when Elizabeth heard the greeting of Mary, the baby leaped in her womb. And Elizabeth was filled with the Holy Spirit, and she exclaimed with a loud cry, "Blessed are you among women, and blessed is the fruit of your womb! And why is this granted to me that the mother of my Lord should come to me? For behold, when the sound of your greeting came to my ears, the baby in my womb leaped for joy. And blessed is she who believed that there would be a fulfillment of what was spoken to her from the Lord." (Luke 1:41–45)

The sound of Mary's salutation was an invitation for faith to come alive. Mary was also pregnant at the time she visited Elizabeth. She was going to give birth to Jesus. The sound of her voice made the baby leap for joy in Elizabeth's belly because she believed that there would be a fulfillment of what the Lord had spoken also. Mary was not only pregnant with a baby who would be named Jesus, she was also overshadowed and filled within her inner being with the Word of God—the fulfillment of the oath that he promised to Abraham and his offspring forever.

In February 1999, my dad went to be with Jesus, and shortly thereafter the news came that I would be a dad myself. It was a shock to me. At the time, my girlfriend, Jenny, and I had just started dating and barely knew each other. There was something about her that I absolutely loved even though our relationship was young. Jenny was beautiful, and she stayed by my side even through my dad's death. When I was on the run, she was the voice of reason telling me to just go home. The one thing I still cherish to this day is her loyalty. She is still standing by my side.

One thing I have realized over time is that the expectancy of what we believe life to be and what it is are two different things. They seem like two speeding locomotives barreling down the same track just waiting to collide. We are often blinded by the fact that heaven and earth interchange on a moment-by-moment basis. There seems to be no warning when it comes, but if we could just slow down we would be able to comprehend the many signs he gives when he calls.

Jenny was about three months pregnant when we had an experience like this. We were headed to work just as we normally would be when our car was struck in the rear quarter panel. The car swerved uncontrollably toward the gas pumps that were near the edge of the road. The music that was blaring in the car seemed silenced as time slowed down. Jenny was even asking why I was driving all over the road. It was then that I saw a huge wing cover the side of the car. The car changed direction and headed away from the pumps into ongoing traffic. Our car struck a truck and came to a complete and abrupt stop.

It is in moments like these that we experience a certain clarity of life. I'm sure you have heard of the expression that life flashes before your eyes during a life-threatening event. Many thoughts went through my mind in the few moments before I heard the sounds of screeching tires and crunching metal. The brevity of life is real, and we are ever so aware of it. Until then I would have been happy to believe that I breathed just to exist and take my small place in this thing called life. I would never have dreamed that, even when bad things happen, God has a greater plan.

After our car finally stopped, I looked over to see if Jenny was all right. Her door was the only one that opened, and she was able to get out of the car on her own. I climbed out through the window on my side of the car and put my feet down on the glass-covered road. As I walked away from the car, I looked back and saw that the only place that wasn't damaged was where we had been sitting. The car looked like an accordion on both sides. We checked to make sure everyone was okay and then sat on the grass in a graveyard and waited for the police and ambulance to come.

As the adrenaline was starting to wear off, I looked over and saw a tombstone with a lamb on top of it. That struck me odd at the time, but it makes perfect sense now. We could hear the sound of the ambulance coming down the road. Many people came over to see if we were okay as we sat there. The only thing I could do was just be thankful that we were alive. It didn't dawn on me at the time to think about the baby that was in Jenny's womb.

When we arrived at the hospital, they rushed her back to check on the baby. Those were some of the longest moments in my life. My heart was not strong enough to endure another loss so soon. As they prepared the ultrasound machine, we awaited for a heartbeat and a good word to say that our baby was okay. A few minutes later we received that peace and assurance. Some would call that a blessing, and it surely was, but I truly believe God demonstrated his grace and mercy to us.

It is in the womb that God births forth his call and his plans over our lives even when we are blind to it. Even at the mention of his Word something takes place from within and begins to go to work from the inside out. Even when we have a bucket full of plans, God brings those plans forth through the shedding of light in our lives and the overshadowing of the Spirit. At his Word, there is something inside that leaps for joy when he begins to help us understand it.

In the book of Samuel we read about a woman by the name of Hannah. She was a woman of deep sorrow and bitterness of soul. The womb is the place where the seed is planted and life comes forth. It is known as the belly or the hollow part of humanity. The womb is the innermost part of a human and is a seat of thought and choice. It is also a place where our words, dreams, and visions are fertilized by the Word of God. Our words are important for this very reason because we can be a well of our words or we can be a wellspring and outflow of God's Word.

The womb can be opened or it can be shut up. Hannah's womb was shut up, and it was a place of unhappiness and grief. As the years went by, she became consumed by her barrenness. Year by year, she became the subject of ridicule. We can become prisoners to our own words. I like to think of our bellies as chambers for our unspoken words. They are the hollow parts of humankind, and they need to be filled with something greater than just our own words. Our words are not only binding agents that can make us feel imprisoned; they are also empowered from on high to loosen us and move us through our troubles. Likewise, on the other hand, we have the authority to bind the strongman of words and thoughts and loosen our living faith with heavenly blessing and the fruit of his Word.

> Or do you not know that your body is a temple of
> the Holy Spirit within you, whom you have from
> God? You are not your own. (1 Corinthians 6:19)

It is a revelation to know that we are not our own and that we were bought at a great but also terrible price. We receive eternal rewards when we understand that our bodies are temples, our hearts are altars, and his Word is our sacrifice. The divine nature is not crafted or devised by man's hand. It is a gift from God that starts in the womb of humankind and is birthed out by his loving nature through grace and truth. It is in this that we see the nature of the seed as it takes up habitation within us.

> The unfolding of your words gives light; it imparts understanding to the simple. (Psalm 119:130)

From the very beginning we can see the nature of his Word. His Word looks into a place of total hollowness and dispels darkness. The entrance of his Word is life, and its framework is our existence. It ushers his presence and fills the empty space with light, revealing its true nature of love. It uncovers all the shadows of our beliefs and births forth a new identity that represents the nature of the seed.

The Word cleaves to the brokenhearted and to the poor in spirit. It gives them a place of comfort and rest and fills them with righteousness. It floods them with mercy and gives them a kingdom and a pure heart. It births a connection between our hearts and the Father's heart. Above all, it gives us entrance to life and a way back to the Father that divulges his true motives, uncovering all darkness and forging forth into the womb a light for the darkness.

Knowing that we are created for a greater purpose in life is a great calling, but knowing that we were called by life itself is beyond words or comprehension. His seed is his voice that connects us to the frequency of heaven and his heart. He gives his Word through practical life experiences sometimes; at other times it seems that he roots deeply in the recesses of our hearts where only he can reach. It is a place that he reserves in our hearts that isn't accessible by anyone but him and his breath. I have learned to cherish this because it is a place where I can be free from the pain, and I can just live.

> The voice of mirth and the voice of gladness, the voice of the bridegroom and the voice of the bride, the voices of those who sing, as they bring thank offerings to the house of the Lord: "Give thanks

to the Lord of hosts, for the Lord is good, for his
steadfast love endures forever!" For I will restore
the fortunes of the land as at first, says the Lord.
(Jeremiah 33:11)

Where there is thanksgiving, there is joy. Up to a certain
point, Hannah had not seen much joy, but she was far from being
finished. She made a vow unto the Lord, and she gave her man-
child who wasn't even born unto the Lord for life. She continued
to pray regardless of the situation that was before her. She began
to speak in her heart; her lips moved, but her voice was not heard.
Even thought to be drunk, she poured out her soul before the
Lord. Only to hear the high priest Eli say, "Go in peace and the
God of Israel grant you the petition that you have asked of him."

Hannah replied, "Let your servant find favor in your eyes."
(1 Samuel 1:18)

At her very words, she went and ate, and she wasn't sad
anymore. Here the word *soul* has many meanings, but the
definition that stands out the most is the seat of emotion or desire.
The Word can and will fill the womb with new life. The thing that
stands in the way is how we are seated, or in other words, how
we are positioned in faith. His Word is absolutely true and never
changes. The thing that changes is the seat or the way we believe.
The game changer is his Word. We don't even have to speak all the
time to see where we are seated. We just have to believe.

The spirit of man is the lamp of the Lord, searching
all his innermost parts. (Proverbs 20:27)

The spirit of humanity is a candle and can be illuminated and
set ablaze by the Spirit of God. It is amazing that we are flesh,
soul, and spirit but presented as one, just as the Lord came in the
flesh, was tempted in all points, and he is spirit but also was one.
It is easy to see him at work as he poured himself out in different

dispensations over time. What is even harder is that he never went anywhere without being one. It has been this way from the very beginning. In every story, we see God at work, we see Jesus at work, and we see the Spirit of God at work all as one. The Word is our perfected bond.

It is in this impartation of light that our eyes are opened to the truth of his Word, and we begin to move as he moves. When we realize we are candles in the hands of a living God, our wombs will be flooded with his light, and the treasures of the dark will appear before our very eyes. Light is a natural agent that stimulates sight and makes things visible. With light we begin to understand the mystery of dark and hidden things. He fashions his Word in humankind and breathes upon it. He frames the way for life and the way into the place of the secret.

The light breaks forth through the outer veil of humankind into the inner and deepest parts. In order for the new person to manifest, the light must pierce the outer veil of the flesh and fill the womb with light. Enlightenment of God's Word stirs the soul while the spirit of the individual is grounded by the truth. The Word is a mirror and often reflects our deepest emotions and causes them to surface or be made manifest. When the deepest things we hold dear surface and come to light, the bands of barrenness are broken off and a deluge of his spirit becomes very evident. These experiences can be hurtful at first, but we are allowed to overcome the hurt. His Word of truth forges the new human to come forth.

> It is the Spirit that gives life; the flesh is no help at all. The words that I have spoken to you are spirit and life. (John 6:63)

Jesus said, "This is why I told you that no one can come to me unless it is granted him by the Father." (John 6:65)

Jesus knew already that unbelief would exist. God's Word is

the catalyst that gives spirit and life. He presented himself here as access to the Father. Truly the Word is our access and makes a way into the present truth of the gospel. Looking at Jesus as the Word that God sent creates a door into the framework of his eternal life and inheritance. We see Jesus not only as written Word but as spoken Word from God coming to rectify the flesh by coming as Son of Man. We also see great demonstration and fulfillment of the Word as Jesus walked and turned no one away. Everywhere he went the light followed and filled.

> Shall I bring to the point of birth and not cause
> to bring forth?" says the Lord; "shall I, who cause
> to bring forth, shut the womb?" says your God.
> (Isaiah 66:9)

In Hannah's case, she was barren and broken before the Lord. She poured herself out before the mercies of God, and he delivered a son named Samuel. Mary would conceive and give birth to Jesus. He was known as the horn of salvation in the house of David. In Mary's case, she was not barren, but she was carrying the seed and first fruit of the birth of many sons. In one case, we see the barrenness of the womb and in another we see the womb at it's most fertile. In the eyes of both women nothing was impossible for God.

The horn symbolized strength and status, and the anointing oil was for the breaking of the yoke. As Hannah prophetically prayed she said, "My heart rejoices in the Lord, mine horn is exalted in the Lord. My mouth is enlarged over mine enemies because I rejoice in thy salvation."

Hannah's countenance changed after her womb was opened and Samuel came forth. Not only was she filled in her womb by a baby, but she also was alive with God's Word because she had been heard, and he had gone forth. When she spoke her innermost desires to God, he spoke his innermost desires through her and revealed the true reflection of her heart to the people. Her heart rejoiced, and her horn was exalted. The horn became her strength and her status. She was no longer her own. Just as she lent Samuel, the Lord lent himself in the flesh to become the answer that Hannah needed.

Hannah brought herself low before the Lord, and he exalted her in due season. Those who are humbled will be exalted. Her tongue was anointed with fresh oil to pull forth the mystery of God and the unlimited anointing over all who were around her. She was planted in the house of the Lord, and there she would flourish and bring forth fruit even in her old age. From there she would be a reflection that God's Word is truth and it is the righteousness of God. Later the Lord came to bless Hannah with three sons and two daughters as his sign of covenant with her.

> "Sing, O barren one, who did not bear; break forth into singing and cry aloud, you who have not been in labor! For the children of the desolate one will be more than the children of her who are married," says the Lord. "Enlarge the place of your tent, and let the curtains of your habitations be stretched out; do not hold back; lengthen your cords and strengthen your stakes." (Isaiah 54:1–2)

The song for those who are barren and need life is a new song. Even though we have felt alone and deserted in the wilderness, God is with us. In brief moments it has felt that he left, but it is his promise to gather us up with great compassion. Even though he hid his face from us, he will not withhold his steadfast love, and he will not remove his covenant of peace. The horn he has given us is a horn of salvation with unlimited anointing, strength, and status. We must sing the new song of the Lamb. We will see the enlargement of our tent and the curtains of your habitation stretching forth. We must not be afraid. We must let go of the old and embrace the new. We must not hold back. The horn is our strength and status in the womb. Cry aloud O barren of God!

On the other hand, Mary would miraculously conceive Jesus. He was the key of David and the seed to many generations forever and ever. There is no end to this kingdom, and it reigns. Before Mary conceived, she also was overflowing in her cup, which spilled over. She magnified the Lord for regarding her in her lowly estate. She called forth the remembrance of his mercy and the seed that was promised to Abraham and his seed forever. Her tongue filled with the enlargement of his kingdom. The birth of Jesus through Mary stretching forth the womb connecting heaven with earth was overshadowed by the spirit, coming first in the womb and then out through her spirit as her lips spoke it. Later, Zechariah, being filled with the Holy Ghost, also prophesied about the horn of salvation being spoken since the world began. Jesus, being the first fruit of many sons, was later given back as our sacrificial Lamb and our way to God.

> Behold, the virgin shall conceive and bear a son, and they shall call his name Immanuel which means God is with us. (Matthew 1:23)

My heart becomes full at the thought of God being with us. When I was sixteen, God began to tug on my heart for the first time. The one thing I can testify is that God is patient and he suffers for long periods of time for the sake of love. I knew he had called me, but I walked in the other direction until I was thirty. I can't begin to describe the emptiness I felt even though my family was always by my side. I was full of dreams and expectations, but I didn't understand what it meant to be full of anything. We can have moments where our best qualities are pinned up on the inside, but eventually they have to come out. The fact is, rather, that whether we are barren or not, the Word of God, known as the seed, is for us.

————◆————

The Word was given to all humankind. I truly believe every person has the potential to unlock God's treasure from deep within, being able to see clearly through the fullness God provided, which is Jesus. A seed planted inside a fertile heart will take root and produce fruit. It's amazing how, when Mary believed the Word of God and submitted herself to his estate, he moved, providing his Word for her to speak, bringing forth Joseph whom she was betrothed to, a place to give birth, and a witness in the earth to the birth of a Messiah.

CHAPTER FOUR

✦━━━━━✦━━━━━✦

His Word, His Will, His Way

M ary gave birth to Jesus and wrapped him in swaddling
clothes and laid him in a manger because there was no
place in the inn. The angel of the Lord appeared unto them, and
the glory of the Lord shone brightly around them as they were
filled by fear.

> The angel said unto them "Fear not, for behold, I
> bring you good news of great joy that will be for
> all the people. For unto you is born this day in
> the city of David a Savior, who is Christ the Lord.
> And this will be a sign for you: you will find a
> baby wrapped in swaddling cloths and laying in a
> manger." (Luke 2:10-11)

It was a sign that the baby was in swaddling clothes and was
lying in a manger. In biblical times, babies were swaddled in long
strips of cloth. The strips were wrapped tightly around the baby
for warmth and to give the baby a sense of security. Even though

Jesus was a baby, he was Immanuel, God with us. Most picture this as Jesus being a baby in a manger, but I like the symbolism here, as he was wrapped in swaddling clothes. To picture the treasure of God wrapped up reminds me of his Word that is buried under the layers of humanity, hidden and accessible only by faith. My second line of thought is that God's sent Word is our warmth and security. Oftentimes, during the most perilous times, his Word swaddled my heart.

Jesus's birth is one the foundations of our faith; it is God's Word becoming flesh and dwelling among us. Without his birth, there would be no Lamb for the sacrifice, and our access to God would be closed off. We wouldn't even be able to approach God without his chosen sacrifice. It is not a coincidence that there was no room in the inn. He was born in a stall made of wood. The wood speaks of humanity and of Christ. What I love about this is that we see the root of Jesse being born and planted in a manger amongst the hay and stubble.

Even when Jesus was in this stage of infancy, we see him planted in the midst of humanity. The seed rooted and became a tree and a sign of the way into life. There are many mentions throughout the scriptures that compare humans being to grass or trees. At Jesus's birth we see a silhouette of God seeding himself into humankind through the form of his fullness and Word, which is Jesus, and then overshadowing and witnessing his birth to the earth through the angel of the Lord. Not only was the tree a way of life, the tree was also used to remove the curse and death of the people. The Word of God makes that way into the arms of the Creator. We would know the meaning of life if we understood the great and terrible price that was paid for that breath.

> Christ redeemed us from the curse of the law by becoming a curse for us. For it is written, "Cursed is everyone who is hanged on a tree." (Galatians 3:13)

Not only did he take the curse for humankind, he also made a way for us to have life without it. Jesus paid for it all. The grass will wither and the flower will fade, but the glory of the Lord will be forever and ever upon those who simply ask for it. He took the tree that was used to curse people and he transformed it into life, the tree of life. I often wondered why Jesus cursed the fig tree on his way to Jerusalem. The fig tree had no fruit ready and available for him. The tree had no life, so it was cursed to die. When a tree has life, it produces fruit. The same is true with the seed. The things that are fruitless are subject to die while the things that have fruit will produce life.

> And when the time came for purification according to the law of Moses, they brought him up to Jerusalem to present him to the Lord (as it is written in the Law of the Lord, "Every male who first opens the womb shall be called holy to the Lord.") (Luke 2:22–23)

Last but not least, when Jesus was born, they took him to Jerusalem for the time of purification according to the Law of the Lord. There was an order of things to be accomplished when he was presented in the temple. The witness of the testimony concerning the Son of God in the earth is the Spirit and the water and the blood. Mary not only gushed forth her testimony, she also gushed forth water and blood from her womb as she gave birth to Jesus in that stall. The imagery of the Lamb of God being born in a manger is beyond words. I want you to see that the gift came down from heaven and it connected with earth.

The order is so imperative. God was the Word or seed. He sent that seed into the earth and used Mary's womb to birth Jesus. He was the tree and the fullness of the fruit all in one. Then the water and blood witnessed to the earth as the Spirit overshadowed the earth. Even the angel of the Lord heralded the good news. Jesus was the first son to be born of many sons making him the first fruit and a way for man to be made in the image and likeness of God. Without God's order, humankind would be lost and couldn't begin to bear what Jesus bore so that we could embrace his likeness.

Jesus was presented in the temple because he was the first of many sons who would open the womb and be called holy of the Lord. He was fully God and fully man. He was born in the Spirit to be God with us. He was born of the flesh to take the curse so that we would have access through its pierced veil. I liken this to Nicodemus and his line of thought.

> Nicodemus said to him, "How can a man be born when he is old? Can he enter a second time into his mother's womb and be born?" Jesus answered, "Truly, truly, I say to you, unless one is born of water and the Spirit, he cannot enter the kingdom of God. That which is born of the flesh is flesh, and that which is born of the Spirit is spirit. Do not marvel that I said to you, 'You must be born again.' The wind blows where it wishes, and you hear its sound, but you do not know where it comes from or where it goes. So it is with everyone who is born of the Spirit." (John 3:4-8)

> For as by a man came death, by a man came also the resurrection of the dead. For as in Adam all die, so also in Christ shall all be made alive. (1 Corinthians 15:21–22)

It is inevitable that there is a seed that is sown into flesh that is flesh. Also there is a seed that is sown into spirit that is Spirit. There was the first man, and his name was Adam. This is the natural body and a living being, and it is subject to corruption because it is earthly, and is made from the dust. Then there was the last Adam who was a life-giving spirit. The first man was from earth while the second was from heaven. This is the beauty and mystery of the Word of God: it becomes, but in you. What is sown is corruptible, but what is raised is incorruptible. What is sown in dishonor; it is raised in glory. What is sown in weakness is raised in power. What is sown a natural body is raised a spiritual body. Those of the dust will resemble and bear the image of the dust while those who are of heaven will be born again and bear the image of the man of heaven. We must put on the incorruptible and the immortality of the living God. We must put on the last man, and his name is Jesus.

> Worthy are you, our Lord and God, to receive glory, honor and power, for you created all things, and by your will they existed and were created. (Revelation 4:11)

The Word of God is the incorruptible seed and the immortality that man seeks, and for that he deserves it all. This is why Jesus had to be born. He is the express image and way back to God. At our word, he takes the corruptible and puts on us the incorruptible. He peels back the layers and opens the veil for us to see the heavenly and the ascended place of rest, the seated place of victory. The only way up is to bow down and ask for him. He will come.

> Therefore, brothers, since we have confidence to enter into the holy places by the blood of Jesus, by a new and living way that he opened for us through the curtain, that is, through his flesh and since we have a great priest over the house of God, let us draw near with a true heart in full assurance of faith, with our heart sprinkled clean from an evil conscience and our bodies washed with pure water. (Hebrews 10:19–22)

We can have this confidence, but only by the one who sacrificed himself so greatly for you and me. The transition is from a living being into a life giving spirit. When we are born again, we should transform from a living being to a life-giving spirit. The confidence comes from our submission to his Word and to his Holy Spirit. When we are living beings, we are capable of sustaining life through the breath that is lent to us from God, but when we are life-giving spirits, the expansion of his heart gushes forth out of us, affecting all who are around us.

The only reason we can be close to God is that we are covered with the blood of his sacrifice, and his flesh became the veil and entrance into a new and living way, turning us from a creature into the arms and heart of a creator. He allows us to draw near to him with a true heart fully assured with faith. Faith is the substance of things hoped for, the evidence of things not seen. Our hearts are sprinkled clean from an evil conscience, and our bodies washed with pure water. The key thing to point out is that, during repentance, our hearts are sprinkled clean from an evil conscience and our bodies are washed with pure water. The word *clean* here means "pure." With this covering we become pure, and that's the thing we need to realize so we can help others with what we have been gifted. It's not of our own, but it is all his.

> Who can say, "I have made my heart pure; I am clean from my sin"? (Proverbs 20:9)

> From that time Jesus began to preach, saying, "Repent, for the kingdom of heaven is at hand." (Matthew 4:17)

Repentance is not only turning away from the life of a living being, it is also coming into a life-giving spirit and the immortality of God—a new and living way consecrated and holy before God. It is walking away from the corruptible and putting on incorruption.

It was not tasked for creation to do this on its own. Christ had to be the Son of Man and be born through the womb because the Word declared it to be so. Christ was holy because he opened the womb and became the first fruit of many sons to be born because the Word said so. Christ was the Word God sent to set free the captive because the Word says so.

The veil or covering served many purposes in the priesthood of the Jewish tradition. All of the furniture in the most holy place was covered before it was moved. Everything inside was holy before God and could not be seen or touched by human hands. The high priest was appointed to the care of holy things inside the temple. It was a duty that wasn't taken lightly and was done soberly and with a great reverence. It was beyond the veil to preserve the way of life. Only those who give their whole heart and life to Jesus have access to this place. When Adam and Eve were put out of the garden, an angel with a flaming sword protected the entrance into the garden, not just to keep them out, but to preserve the way of life.

> And the Lord God made for Adam and his wife garments of skins and clothed them. (Genesis 3:21)

It is amazing how infinite God's mercy is displayed even from the very beginning. Right after Adam and Eve were put out of the garden, we see the shadow of the covering, which I believe to be the second man, Jesus.

His tender mercies were on display as he covered their nakedness. When we are born into this world, we come into it as living beings. We are naked until we are cleaned off and then covered. The same is true in God's kingdom. We have to be born again to be cleaned up and covered. Then and only then can we be a life-giving spirit to others because we reflect the true nature of Father.

God walked with Adam and Eve in the midst of the garden. It was the true essence of communion. They were commanded not to eat of the tree of the knowledge of good and evil. At this time, they weren't even aware of their nakedness because it was a place unhindered and unveiled where they walked with God in all his splendor. They were simply in a place where God was with them, and this place was fully furnished with everything they needed. Then they were deceived by the serpent. They ate from the tree, and their eyes were opened to the world and the corruptible nature.

This led to Adam having to sweat from his brow to contend for the seed, and Eve having to feel the pains of childbirth. The incorruptible seed was sent by God and was God. The only thing God requires for the new nature is submission and faith. It is a fully furnished work prepared for you and me, and it is a blueprint for the entrance and the way into life. Eating from the tree of the knowledge of good and evil will lead into corruption and away from life. It leads you in a way that seems right, but in the end it is sweaty and awfully painful and provides minimal results from the seed bringing forth fruit.

The natural body has physical senses that guide it in the way of good and evil, but a regenerated spirit guides us in faith toward the knowledge of his Word and the way of life. It brings us back to the heart of a loving Father. In the garden the serpent appealed to Adam and Eve's senses and questioned God's Word by twisting it and presenting it in a different way. I am convinced it has always been God's plan to be with us, but it simply comes back to what seed we choose.

> I put on righteousness, and it clothed me; my
> justice was like a robe and a turban. (Job 29:14)

After Adam and Eve ate the fruit and failed God, their eyes were opened. They knew they were naked and sewed fig leaves together to make aprons to cover their nakedness. Then, after the curse was pronounced, because of disobedience, the Lord God made them coats of skins and clothed them. This is the first time we see God and his righteousness on display covering the shame and the nakedness that sin brings forth. Although the ground became riddled with thistles and thorns and childbirth became painful, God never failed them. Death was even introduced, but God was certain to make a way.

After they ate from the tree, we get a clear picture of the blessed and the cursed with Cain and Abel. The one thing that stands out the most is the definition of good and evil. One thing is true even to this day. When we eat of this tree, it brings forth the knowledge of good and evil. The corruptible seed will bring forth the fruit of corruption. In the corruptible seed, it seems that we are participating in a balancing act between good and evil driven by our feelings and our seat of emotions, while eating from the incorruptible makes a clear path to the way and life itself.

I want you to take notice that Eve conceived and bore Cain first. The symbolism here is that Cain was the first and a tiller of the ground. It is a picture of the first human—a human made from the dust. Even in the process of time, he brought forth fruit from the ground to be an offering to the Lord. Cain did not respect the offering and became very angry, and his countenance fell. Cain talked with Abel and rose up and killed him. Cain was cursed and driven out from the face of the earth as a fugitive and a vagabond. Cain's punishment was more than he could bear, so the Lord set a mark upon him. Vengeance would be taken out sevenfold for whoever would slay Cain.

The mark that God gave Cain was a reminder that we must never take out vengeance on each other. When we do this, we help darkness multiply, and we shed the blood of the innocent. From the blood of Abel to the blood of Zechariah, the son of Barachiah who was murdered between the sanctuary and the altar, we see the blood of righteous men before God who were greatly honored, but they were only righteous because of God's righteousness and his great sacrifice. As for the darkness without a sacrifice of his righteousness, the blood of righteous men comes down on the heads of evil men causing a vicious cycle for generations to come.

> Deliver me from blood guiltiness, O God, O God
> of my salvation, and my tongue will sing aloud of
> your righteousness. (Psalm 51:14)

Even when men were given the choice of Barabbas or Jesus, they chose Barabbas. It was innocent blood or guilty blood. Jesus stood before the people silent and scourged, as a lamb going to the slaughter. He was perfectly justified and in one accord with heaven. He was honorable and true to the point of scourging and even unto imminent and sure death through the bearing of a tree but he remained unmoved and upright.

They cried aloud, "We want Barabbas! Crucify Jesus!

Pontius Pilate asked, "What evil has he done?"

They cried even louder saying, "Let him be crucified!"

The mark of vengeance cries aloud for false justice while passing down the sentence of blood guilt. It cries louder and louder until judgment is passed and completely fulfilled. It strips justice and crowns it with thorns. It spits and mocks as it passes by wagging its head.

It declares, "His blood be on us and our children!" (Matthew 27:25)

This is why he never left vengeance to humankind. Vengeance requires immediate retribution, and the price is more than we can pay. The shoulders of humankind weren't meant to bear the burdens that vengeance requires. This is one of the main reasons that we have to identify with him and be available for his yoke. Cain was angry, and his countenance fell at his sacrifice. The image that we reflect is like fruit that comes forth in season, starting with the seed, then the roots, and after that, the manifestation of the seed and its fruit. The seed that we sow makes all the difference in the way we grow. If we sow the seeds of the knowledge of good and evil, we will bring forth a seat that is earthly, while sowing God's seed will bring forth a seat of the heavenly.

> By faith Abel offered to God a more acceptable sacrifice than Cain, through which he was commended as righteous, God commending him by accepting his gifts. And through his faith, though he died, he still speaks. (Hebrews 11:4)

Abel was a keeper of sheep. He brought forth the firstlings of his flock and of the fat thereof. The Lord had respect unto Abel and his offering. It was pleasing to the Lord. His sacrifice was offered to God and was commended as righteous because of his faith. His blood cried from the ground. Even after he died, he still spoke.

You might ask, "How can one who died speak?"

I truly believe he had a voice that identified with another, and it was through his faith that his blood cried out from the earth, and God heard. We see a picture that speaks loudly even after death. I am reminded that we overcome by the blood of the Lamb and by the Word of our testimony, loving not our lives unto death. Even after death faith rings loudly in face of darkness and it cries for mercy. There is only the blood of one that makes the blood of many speak, and that is the blood of Jesus.

God used Abel to display a powerful act of unity between heaven and earth. God is the keeper of the flock, and he brought forth the firstling of the flock and the fat thereof. The firstling of the flock was Jesus, also known as the Word of God. The offering of God toward humankind commended the sacrifice as righteous through the faith of the believing. Abel cried out to God because of faith in his sacrifice. His offering of faith produced righteousness because it was of God and was God. It was simply giving back what God had given, and that was himself. Faith produces the work of God, which is to simply believe. When we believe, we will be compelled to move.

The word *commend* simply means to praise formally or officially. It is an act of honor and a compliment to give back to God what he has so graciously given, and it is the only acceptable gift. Commend also means to entrust someone or something to. He commended his love toward us while we were still sinners. God is love, so he entrusted his Word to humankind. He gave Jesus to us, and that is a picture of life and love. There is only one who gave himself for humankind, and his name is Jesus. There are many gods and many idols, but only one way and one truth back to God, and that is through his Son, Jesus. He is our salvation and so much more than we can comprehend.

God's faithfulness is limitless. He supplies himself from faith to faith and from word to word. In this we see the righteousness of God becoming light before our very eyes. He comes line upon line and precept upon precept until he opens the eyes of our understanding and circumcises our hearts with truth. It is in this truth that the commendation comes written, not in ink or on stones, but on the fleshly tablets of the heart scribed and witnessed by the Spirit of the Living God.

> For I am not ashamed of the gospel, for it is the power of God for salvation to everyone who believes, to the Jew and also to the Greek. For in it the righteousness of God is revealed from faith to faith. As it is written, "The righteous shall live by faith." (Romans 1:16–17)

Faith is the substance of things that are hoped for and the evidence of things not seen. The gospel is the power of God for salvation to all who believe because it is a living Word. The power of the gospel is pure and transforming for all who encounter it. It is God's treasure and his plan of hope. It is not only written, but it lives through Christ and is witnessed by the Spirit of God to all who are yoked with it. In his gospel you will find the solution to every problem. When we submit to his Word through faith, the invisible attributes become reality. His eternal power and his divine nature have been clearly perceived from the time of creation because there will be no other way to enter except through God's Word, which is Jesus.

The creatures of the earth were called from the utter darkness of the depths for one purpose, and that was to glorify the Creator. It was clearly perceived because, from the beginning, the purpose of creatures is to return to the Creator. I believe this has never changed. This is and will always be the plan. I believe darkness continues to live because we, as humankind, forget to give what is due to God, and that is his glory. He gave his breath for humankind as he stooped down to the earth and breathed life. I believe with all my heart that we should spend our whole lives giving that back to him.

Abel's blood crying out was an establishment of faith for righteous blood. It was his witness. It is not what we do that makes us righteous; rather, it is the one who covers us. The establishment of covenant started at the beginning of time when God made a way for humans to see life. He started looking into darkness and calling forth light and life to a garden, then in an ark, and, lastly, in us. Although the substance that he uses is completely different, the pattern remains the same with God above all, Jesus as his Word in the earth, and the Spirit overshadowing or covering the work. This is an establishment of righteousness that was forged only by God alone. It is in his incorruptible seed with the overshadowing of all of heaven as witness.

The cry of Abel was just the first of many righteous people who called out from the blood of one and the seat of the heavenly. Even though his blood cried out from the earth, he was heard in heaven because he gave God what was due. Also it was the cries of innocent blood that appealed to the mercies of God. It was those tender mercies that allowed Adam to know his wife again.

Adam knew his wife again and conceived a son in his likeness and image and named him Seth. The name Seth in Hebrew means "appointed." Seth would later also have a son, and he would be named Enos, which means "mortal." On the day God created man, he made him in his own likeness. He created male and female and called their name Adam in the day they were created. Adam was the first man, natural and of the earth. We see these men in the godly lineage of Jesus in the gospel of Luke. Adam was a living soul, and those who followed after him were appointed and mortal.

The reason I say *appointed* and *mortal* is that even to this day each member of humankind is appointed to follow after God with all his or her being and to become more and more each day into the likeness of his Word. Even in the face of darkness multiplying and the limitations of this natural body, we are called to become greater through him who calls us. As he maximizes we minimize. I want you to think on it this way: when he increases, we decrease. His Word is the empowerment to the believer. Every answer we will ever seek in life lies right before us in plain and clear view. With every breath there is a revealing of Jesus, God's Word in the earth and in humankind.

> Then the Lord said, "My Spirit shall not abide in
> man forever, for he is flesh" (Genesis 6:3).

The flesh is a covering for humankind and is subject to mortality. Mortality is the state of being subject to death. This is why God covered Adam and Eve after they tried to cover themselves with fig leaves. Flesh reveals the nakedness of humankind, and mortality brings forth death. He was preserving the way of life. The flesh is perishable and delicate. They were beguiled by their words because, at that moment, they became aware of the knowledge of good and evil. When God called to his creation, Adam was afraid and naked. He hid himself. With this being said, we see the nature and condition of humankind with his own words. The knowledge of good and evil will bring forth a very similar word that sounds like God's Word, but in the end it brings forth death.

———◆———

There is a time for everything. In Adam, humankind is appointed to the toils of good and evil even being subject to death. He is subject to the toils of his hands and the sweat of his brow where the ground is unfertile. The increase of fruit is far and in between. He is also subject to the seed and fruit that come from his words. In Adam's nature, our words are a place of work and sweat with small yields of perishable fruit.

There is a need to see Adam for who he is. Adam walked and talked with God, and it was a pure connection. When Adam failed to keep the garden, he was subject to his own words and the results that followed. It was sin that followed.

CHAPTER FIVE

Redemptive Nature of the Living Word

Therefore, as one trespass led to condemnation
for all men, so one act of righteousness leads to
justification and life for all men.

—Romans 5:18

T he barrier between humankind and God is sin. Sin happened
when the pure connection was interrupted by the corruption
of words. The heavenly realm and the earthly realm are connected
by words. Sin leads to condemnation, which simply means the
pronouncement of being guilty and expressing unfavorable or
adverse judgment or censure. The one trespass of Adam led to the
condemning of all men. The trespass was that he broke that pure
connection with God. In other words, he severed the bond that
God made through the agreement of other words.

The only thing that stops humankind today from realizing the
truth of righteousness is that they fail to see the obedience of the
sacrifice. One act of righteousness leads to justification and life for
all people. It was a sacrifice that was forged by the fire of his own

Word and the blood of a pure Lamb. By this one action he justified humankind through the sacrifice of his Son, Jesus. Life comes on greater measures when we are aware of the obedience of the sacrifice. His obedience to be our sacrifice is the demonstration of his Word. Our obedience is wrapped up in one Word, and that's the Word of God.

> And so, from the day we heard, we have not ceased to pray for you, asking that you may be filled with the knowledge of his will in all spiritual wisdom and understanding, so as to walk in a manner worthy of the Lord, fully pleasing to him: bearing fruit in every good work and increasing in the knowledge of God; being strengthened with all power, according to his glorious might, for all endurance and patience with joy; giving thanks to the Father, who has qualified you to share in the inheritance of the saints in light. He has delivered us from the domain of darkness and transferred us to the kingdom of his beloved Son, in whom we have redemption, the forgiveness of sins. (Colossians 1:9–14)

It starts with the Word of God. Even from the beginning we see the preeminence of God's Word as he spoke it out into the darkness and things just "became." Christ was preeminent, and he was the image of the invisible God and the firstborn of many sons to come from the dead. Preeminence is the fact of surpassing all others. It is superior to all things and shows greatness and excellence. The Word of God is distinct from all other words because it ushers the life of God not only in written form but in his Spirit and his truth. This is why they called him Immanuel, which means God is with us. His Word is ever so present, and it is breath and life in a dark place.

His preeminence was in creation as the Word of God created the heavens and the earth forming the visible and the invisible. He was before all things, and all things exist for his good pleasure. He was the head and the fullness of all good things that were, and are, and ever will be. There was nothing before him. He was the beginning and the hope we attach our faith to. He is the Father of lights, and he delivered us from the power of darkness, translating us in the kingdom of his Son. He forges light into darkness, uncovering the mystery of his kingdom through the power and demonstration of his Word.

Uncovering redemption lies in the mystery of his Word. The word *redemption* means the action of being saved. It also means regaining possession of something in exchange for payment. Before we can actually regain something, it has to be lost, being torn loose from mortality and redeemed with immortality. Our lives are delivered from the enslavement of bondage from the knowledge of good and evil by the redemptive release of a newfound freedom by the sacrifice of Jesus Christ. In his Word we see both ideas. We see deliverance and the cost that was paid for it. Redemption comes to us through great sacrifice and the warm flow of his blood. The power of the testimony doesn't come from looking up or down but from looking deep within ourselves and finding the redemption that God planted in us. Although it is buried under layers and layers of flesh, the Spirit of God reveals itself through his Word and his blood. His blood speaks to ours.

> For even the Son of Man came not to be served but to serve, and to give his life as a ransom for many." (Mark 10:45)

Jesus became the Son of Man not to be ministered to but to minister to the people and give his life for many as a ransom for the price of death. The word *ransom* also means "to release with a payment." Jesus was the payment for sin. The eternal reward of life comes forth only through him. Not only does he characterize redemption, he also becomes flesh to minister redemption to the people and to become their redemption. He was sent to be redemption unto the people and to be a demonstration of his covenant of life that is forever. His name is holy and should be reverenced in all the earth.

> He is clothed in a robe dipped in blood, and the name which he is called is the Word of God. (Revelation 19:13)

I find it interesting that the psalmist declares, "For you have exalted above all things your name and your word." (Psalm 138:2)

Here we see a magnification of his Word above his name. Redemption is creative because it takes the testimony of God for humankind to overcome and the covering of blood to be able to stand and walk uprightly before him.

I truly believe his name is above all other names, and there is no other that could rival it. Magnification of his Word comes at the sound of his name. It's learning that when we speak his name the fullness of his Word follows. Whenever I have tried to understand the solution to any of my problems and I've needed an answer, his name has always been my outlet and beginning of understanding. Directly after that, his Word follows in fullness of life.

There is a manner that is worthy of the Lord, and the standard of it starts at the utterance of his name and his Word. His Word leaves us with the hope of being filled with the knowledge of his will. In his Word we are fully pleasing to him with endless possibilities of bearing fruit and increasing in every good work in the knowledge of God. His Word qualifies us and positions us for eternal inheritance. He prepares our hearts to endure in patience with an earnest expectation of joy. He strengthens the heart with all power according to his glorious might, delivering those in darkness and translating us into the kingdom of his beloved Son. It's in him that we begin to understand his redemption and his plan for the forgiveness of sins. It's not only understanding redemption but also knowing we are the redeemed and a portrait of redemption for those who need it.

There are so many great stories of redemption in the Word of God. I would like to start with Moses in the book of Exodus. It is truly amazing that God shows up miraculously in the midst of our situations just as he did for Moses. It is absolutely ridiculous to understand that God can use the same hand that persecutes us to favor us even in the midst of great persecution. The Israelites were in a time of great multiplication and fruitfulness, but a new king was rising to power. His plans were to set upon them taskmasters to afflict them with their burdens and eventually to kill all males by casting them in the river. It was also a plan of extinction imposed on the Israelites because the pharaoh of Egypt set forth the command to kill every Hebrew male. At this point the Passover had not yet come, but God worked from the shadows and caused light to spring forth. He works in the places where our feet are not able to tread and bridges the gap between the chasm and a beautiful existence created for you and me. He causes redemption and life to come from grips of death. That Passover resulted in humankind not receiving death for eternity but being sanctified by the covering of blood and water through the matrix of life. This was a witness to the earth of God's kingdom.

There was an order spoken by the king of Egypt to the Hebrew midwives concerning the firstborn males. The midwives names were Shiphrah and Puah. The Hebrew meaning of *Shiphrah* is "beauty" while *Puah* is defined as "radiance" in the sense of light. There is beauty and radiance in the first covenant that Moses would soon give to the people. The midwives feared God and didn't listen to the command of the king of Egypt.

When asked why they did not obey, they replied, "Because the Hebrew women are not like the Egyptian women, for they

are vigorous and give birth before the midwife comes to them."
(Exodus 1:19)

> Blessed be the God and Father of our Lord Jesus
> Christ! According to his great mercy, he has caused
> us to be born again to a living hope through the
> resurrection of Jesus Christ from the dead, to an
> inheritance that is imperishable, undefiled, and
> unfading, reserved in heaven for you, who by
> God's power are being guarded through faith for
> a salvation ready to be revealed in the last time.
> (1 Peter 1:3–5)

Here we see the Word of God as a gift that is given as a living
hope. As in birth, the Word comes forth in all beauty and radiance.
At every act of faith, a new view of brilliance comes forth revealing
more of himself. When the midwives feared God, it was an act of
faith that brought wisdom and strength even in great oppression. At
the midwives' obedience to fear God, he made them houses, or in
other words, he gave them families. He multiplied the people greatly.
Children are God's heritage, and the fruit of the womb is his reward.

The word *heritage* is defined as property—physical or
intellectual—that may be inherited. It can be a special or individual
possession or an allotted portion that is passed down through
generations. This is truly one of the most sacred of things, but
God gave his Son, Jesus, as a heritage to humankind—a lively hope
through a living Word passed down from generation to generation.
The fear of God is the beginning of wisdom. It multiplies greatly
in fruitfulness and a goodly heritage. It was God's plan from the
foundation of the earth to build his Word through faith first
spoken then demonstrated.

> Unless the Lord builds the house, those who build
> it labor in vain. (Psalm 127:1)

Without his living Word we become fruitless, portraying an image of self. His heritage is his Word, and it is spotless and blameless, preserving the heart from within. Without a sacrifice of living Word upon the altar of the heart, we are left with the vices of our vanity looking inward in search for help. I have found that there are situations beyond our reasoning and control. Our words carry great power, and there are many men and women to prove that throughout history supporting a legacy of words that stand in the world for many years to come. There are also many men and women who have a living hope through the resurrection of Jesus Christ, the incarnate Word of God—a God-given inheritance that is imperishable and undefiled, unfaded, and reserved in heaven by God's power guarded by faith for a salvation to be revealed in the last time.

It is without a shadow of a doubt that the Egyptians in this time were a power and force to be reckoned with. Even as the midwives stood before Pharaoh and heard his command, they feared God and saved the male children anyway. They were witness to this lively hope and the heritage that would come years later. There is something about birth that puts life into perspective. Even in this we can see the way of life being guarded and preserved as the midwives were obedient to the call of the firstborn. All things work together for those who love God. Even in the midst of great travail and groaning, God would hear them and be reminded of his covenant with them.

> Now the point in what we are saying is this: we have such a high priest, one who is seated at the right hand of the throne of the Majesty in heaven, a minister in the holy places, in the true tent that the Lord set up, not man. For every high priest is appointed to offer gifts and sacrifices; thus it is necessary for the priest to have something to offer. Now if he were on earth, he would not be

priest at all, since there are priests who offer gifts
according to the law. They serve a copy or shadow
of heavenly things. For when Moses was about
to erect a tent, he was instructed by God, saying,
"See that you make everything according to the
pattern that was shown to you on the mountain"
(Hebrews 8:1–6).

We often see Moses as the one whom God called as the
mediator of the old covenant and the deliverer of his people. We
could also see him as a servant for a copy or shadow of heavenly
things. In the beginning of the book of Exodus, we see the baby
Moses in an ark of bulrushes coated in slime. He was set on the
brink of the river, waiting for Pharaoh's daughter to draw him out
and give him back to his mother to nurse. Moses was a man, but
he was orphaned and learned the ways of the Egyptians. We are
also called to serve as a copy or shadow of heavenly things. We
are to be so transparent that people see the true high priest and
tent, which is Jesus.

And Moses was instructed in all wisdom of
the Egyptians, and he was mighty in deed and
in words. When he was forty years old, it came
into his heart to visit his brothers, the children of
Israel. (Acts 7:22–23)

An obvious part of life is being born into it, our flesh being
a tent for the true spirit that dwells inside. At some point in
life everyone is faced with the question of creation. Moses was
instructed by the Egyptians for forty years, but the reins of his
heart were being pulled on by God. The Egyptians served many
gods and many temples, but the heart of God desires that you
serve him with one true heart aligned to one true God. Our tent
here on earth, or our flesh, serves as a shadow of heavenly things.

Our hearts should reflect the nature of a true and living God. Just like the heart that pumps blood and life throughout the flesh, the Word of God pumps life and blood to all it covers. It is a covering for the heart of humankind ushering in a kingdom that doesn't come from an up-and-down position, but from within.

Even though Moses was mighty in words and deeds according to the Egyptians, there was still a pull in his heart. I believe that every person, at some point in time, has this pull, but it's how we respond to it that is most important. After Moses was grown and his heart was bent toward his brethren, he looked upon them in their burdens and was distraught. He even tried to redeem them as he slew an Egyptian, but he found that Pharaoh would not be merciful in his cause. He fled from Pharaoh in the face of vengeance. Redemption doesn't flow from the seat of vengeance; rather, it flows from a seat of mercy.

We look at the Word of God as a weapon that slays the enemy and takes vengeance on the wicked. The Word of God is a sword that is quick and powerful. It pierces, dividing asunder of soul and spirit, and joints and marrow. His Word is the discerner of thoughts and intents of the heart. I believe Moses fled from Pharaoh for his life but also because his heart was exposed and manifested before God. There is not one creature that is not manifest in his sight. We are naked and opened unto the eyes of our Creator. One of the greatest revelations we could ever receive is that, without him, we can do merely nothing. The new life starts when our hearts are opened to him, and we cannot do this without his Word.

I have often asked God, "Why do we flee?"

Over time I have come to the conclusion that we can never escape the inevitability of God's Word. This is why Jesus is the Word of God and the only way to God. The pre-incarnate work was valuable substance from the very beginning and is still today. The word *pre-incarnate* is defined as having existence before incarnation. The word *pre-incarnate* is used especially of the second person of the Trinity. The Word of God not only took on flesh, it also revealed its true nature to humankind, suffering this world and the brutality of the cross.

The incarnation of Christ is the Word of God becoming flesh for you and me. He is the only begotten of the Father, and he is full of grace and truth. It has taken me years of looking at the Word of God to see the fullness of his grace and truth, and some days I believe I'm just at the tip of the iceberg. He became flesh and dwelled among us. I believe he still does through the life and law of the Holy Spirit. I believe he is ever so near to us every waking moment of the day. The exchange of heaven and earth happens when he gives us life in this flesh—not ours, but his. In the everlasting communion of bread and wine, the bread is his flesh and the wine is his Spirit. In this we have a knowledge of he who called us, and we are governed by the Spirit concerning his will. His will is clearly stated in the Word of God. It's in this we see all three come together as one.

> Where shall I go from your Spirit? Or where shall
> I flee from your presence? (Psalm 139:7)

When the flesh of man is not willing to accept the sacrifice, it flees from the truth, wandering in the wilderness accepting the ways that it simply knows. Moses was trained up in the way of the Egyptians. Then he had a tug on his heart. We cannot ignore when God pulls on the reins of the heart. Moses murdered the man who oppressed God's people, and then he hid the matter in the sand. At the time, that was Moses's nature. The nature of the creature is to hide the matter, but the nature of God is to reveal fully. It was the nature of creature, flesh, and mortality that fled into the wilderness where he dwelt in the land of Midian. It was the nature of God to reveal his purpose to Moses even in the wilderness. It is at the end of man that God will miraculously appear.

The psalmist David said it like this: "If I ascend to heaven, you are there! If I make my bed in hell, you are there! If I take the wings of the morning and dwell in the uttermost parts of the sea, even there your hand shall lead me, and your right hand shall hold me." (Psalm 139:8)

The place name Midian has come to mean a place of judgment. Judgment is the ability to make considered decisions or come to sensible conclusions. The thoughts and the ways of the Lord are higher. There is nothing more considered or sensible than the Word of God. It is set as a standard for humankind to supply the present help for the time at hand. It was not suffered to be abused by humankind, but to simply reveal the truth and manner of humankind and each member's heart. Moses found this out as he fled from the face of Pharaoh into the wilderness of Midian. We can flee to the ends of the earth, but even into eternity he will ever be so present.

After seeing one of his brethren suffered wrong, Moses defended and avenged him who was oppressed. Vengeance brings forth misunderstanding amongst brethren. It causes questions to arise about the condition of our ability to lead and judge. Vengeance clouds our ability to love and forgive. These are two very essential parts of the gospel. We can lead and judge only by the standard of God's Word and the discerning of the Spirit. Vengeance can drive us out into a vast wilderness, but God always has a way of reaching his creations.

Moses came to the mountain of God when the angel of the Lord appeared unto him in a flame of fire out of the midst of a bush. It's hard to imagine a pure flame that burns intensely but doesn't consume what it burns. It is definitely a sight that would make our heads turn around so we could look. Even when God called to Moses, he heard the voice and was able to answer it without completely understanding it. He was drawn by something that had been planted in him from the time of his very own creation.

God called unto him and said, "Moses, Moses!" and he said, "Here I am." (Exodus 3:4)

It is easy to say that this is a learned behavior. When I was a child, I would wait by the door and watch the driveway, waiting for my dad to come home. He worked a lot to provide for our family, but he always made time for us. We can say this was learned because there are things in life that are habit forming. I believe also that there is a higher place than emotion and habit that drives us into faith. It wasn't about waiting for my dad to just see him; it was hearing his voice and knowing who he was. When I heard that voice I knew he was the man of the house and his provision was mine because he had worked dearly for it. I knew his love and comfort with that voice. I also knew that there should be a reverence for those who provide. It seems that, in some points of the journey, we are just waiting for that reassuring voice of comfort and provision.

God, our Father, is holy and must be reverenced. His comfort and provision are his Word. It is a complete blueprint of life. In order to be fulfilled, we have to be able to accept God's way and his will. That means submitting ourselves to him. After years of being under his care, I have come to the realization that he called me. I didn't call upon him first, but he called me. We have to accept the fact that he is holy and to be reverenced. The amazing part about God is that he shares his provisions even when we don't deserve them. It's in this that we see his goodness. It leads to repentance or a turning to God.

When we are in the place of his presence we stand on holy ground. Where he is, there is the kingdom, the power, and the glory forever and ever.

Through faith, we understand that the worlds were framed by his Word. It is in this place of understanding that we will gladly remove our shoes and be girded with something greater, having our feet shod with the preparation of the gospel of peace. His Word also prepares our feet for the place of his presence. He gives us the boldness of the approach to the throne of grace that we might obtain mercy and find grace to help in our time of need. It is a great reminder of when I waited for Dad at the door. He would pull up and get out of the car. He would just motion with his arms, and I would run into them.

The first time God called my name, I hid my face and was afraid to look upon him. It took me fourteen long and trying years in the wilderness to understand even one of God's basic precepts: simply that he loved me regardless and that he had called me.

I mustered up the strength and asked, "Who am I?"

I had tried everything else outside the gates of hell. I have a hard time believing I could even muster any strength at all. I remember putting my head between my hands and thinking that I had tried everything in my own power, and I needed help. I had many excuses and arguments with God about the call, but I believe firmly that he equips and commissions the called. As soon as I admitted I needed help, he was there. He sent many my way with his Words to encourage. Faith comes by hearing, and hearing by the Word. His Word musters the strength that lies deep within. When we listen to it, faith arises. Also we acquire our sense to hear by the Word as we learn that the place on which we stand is holy ground. Wherever his Word is, he is!

The Word of God stirs up the deep wells of faith from within. The ability to hear is a gift. Faith is drummed up as we sit under the Word. Faith opens up the ears to hear what he is saying. I spent fourteen years in the wilderness because I heard the words God was speaking but truly wasn't hearing them. Another way to say it is to receive the words.

But Moses said to the Lord, "Oh, my Lord, I am not eloquent, either in the past or since you have spoken to your servant, but I am slow of speech and of tongue." (Exodus 4:10)

It is amazing that the gift of hearing comes before the gift of speech. If we cannot hear what he is saying, we cannot speak what he is saying. Not only being able to receive but to give what you received is key. The time that we spend in his presence is vital. It is always a place where we are quick to hear and slow to speak. It is also holy and reverenced. This is why humility is required. It is a place for instruction, not only for us but also for all those who are around us.

> I will instruct you and teach you in the way you
> should go. I will counsel you with my eye upon
> you. (Psalm 32:8)

The Lord can give his counsel even through the most doubtful men. There are many chosen by God who were flawed beyond measure. The true measure is the inward appearance, which humankind has no way of seeing for certain. The Lord searches the heart and tests the mind. He gives to humankind according to each person's ways and according to the fruit of each person's deeds. The motives and ways of humankind are ever before God. The scriptures are breathed out by God to equip humankind for every good work. Even the most intelligent of humankind can be wrong about the scriptures. I believe this is why we have to be good listeners. He's the only one that knows our true hearts' conditions.

God knew the heart of Moses. He knows the hearts of all people whether we admit it or not. God called from the burning bush, and Moses answered. I believe we will all have that opportunity at some point in time. It is an impossible thing to enter into his presence when the only thing we know is judgment. God surely is the righteous judge of all his creation, but he is also patient. He waits for creation and longs for the day when creation will do anything to be in his presence, even when we are afraid to look upon him and things don't seem right. I have learned that no matter where I am in life, he is there. He is the answer to everything that pertains to this life and beyond.

It is impossible for humankind alone to accomplish the works of God. He draws us through faith to believe in the impossible. He creates in us with His Word. He makes the impossible become possible. It was impossible for Moses to come onto the mount in his condition. He had spent forty years in Egypt, and then forty more in the wilderness. He was in a place of running and judgment when God called from the burning bush and Moses answered. At his voice we come alive and begin to learn the purpose and will of God upon our lives.

But Moses said to God, "Who am I that I should go to Pharaoh and bring the children of Israel out of Egypt?" God said to Moses, "I am who I am." And he said, "Say this to the people of Israel: 'I am has sent me to you.'" (Exodus 3:11, 14)

We have to see that humankind will come to the end of the rope. It's just not the end, however, but only the beginning. When we have nothing else to say, God will speak on our behalf. Even in Moses's unperfected state, God's Word found the place in his repentant heart. Moses was a stranger in a strange land, but he was never far from the promise. God would search the earth for just one who would humble down before him to receive the engrafted Word. It is not that God hasn't spoken; it is that sometimes we fail to hear him.

> When Moses saw it, he was amazed at the sight, and as he drew near to look, there came the voice of the Lord. "I am the God of your fathers, the God of Abraham and of Isaac and of Jacob." And Moses trembled and did not dare to look. (Acts 7:31–32)

———◆———

The Word of God reveals the true nature of God. It also reveals the nature of humankind and the condition of the heart. His Word sheds light upon the darkest place. The heart of humankind can be one of the darkest places. It is a hidden place to all others but God. He always sees our true motives. The heart is a seat of thoughts and emotion. It is often masked by our flesh. It reasons and ponders the ways of life. The hearts of humankind reveal the true individual through the fruit of his or her lips. The heart is the center of humankind. It can be a seat of thoughts and emotion or it can be a seat of faith building the kingdom of God from within.

CHAPTER SIX

God Knows...Even in Our Struggle

Now some of the scribes were sitting there,
questioning in their hearts.

—*Mark 2:6*

We have the ability to reason within our hearts. The human heart can be driven by emotions and thoughts. It is out of the heart that flows the issues of life. It is in the humility of the heart that we begin to operate in faith. It goes far beyond reasoning into the unknown where we begin to trust God at his Word. We have to be able to surrender our hearts, which are full of thoughts and emotions, for something much greater, but this requires humility and the willingness to move forward. There are many times I have tested the Word of God, and it has led me to trust him more because he always performs his Word.

And immediately Jesus, perceiving in his spirit
that they thus questioned within themselves, said

to them, "Why do you question these things in
your hearts?" (Mark 2:8)

We see a perfect example of Jesus, the Word of God, perceiving
the questionings in the hearts of those gathered. Again the Word
of God is always discerning the thoughts and intentions of the
heart, piercing to the division of soul and of spirit. Even though
Jesus is standing before them, he is demonstrating that he is the
Word by knowing the thoughts and intentions of their hearts. He
knows that they struggle in their hearts with the question, but he
is ever so near to present the truth.

We often mask the truth with feelings. We cover our hearts
with everything else but the truth. The struggle is certainly real
while we're in the midst of it. Sometimes it seems easier to mask
the pain and carry the load, but our shoulders were never built to
carry the weight of the world. The heart can often be deceptive,
fooling the senses and driving us into a vast wilderness of sweat,
blood, and tears. All the while, God waits for us patiently, taking
it all step by step and breath by breath.

He prepares our hearts to come boldly unto his grace. God's
grace for us is Jesus. One of the synonyms for God's grace is God's
reward at Christ's expense. God enables us to obtain the mercy
and grace in a time of our need. When we begin to trust God, he
becomes the supplication of our hearts. His Word begins to be
our humble plea. From the very beginning of creation the greatest
gift to us has been the Word. Jesus was full of grace and truth. He
certainly has the ability not only to be written about so his story can
be passed on throughout the ages, but he can demonstrate himself
in the fullness of grace and truth. He becomes it from within.

It is obvious that we will always have the will to choose, and
that's when the struggle becomes real. Our choices in words
become the fruit for us later and demand the truth. We assimilate
with our words to the point that they become a rooted reality. We
take them in and make them part of a larger thing. Words cause us

to expand and adopt ideas, becoming a part of the bigger picture. Before long, we begin to believe the words we speak, and then we become as them. Words can be freeing or they can confine like a prison. I believe this is why God cautioned Moses as he looked at the flame. God's presence is a holy place. We must be able to count the cost of his Word. Although Moses wasn't fully aware of the cost, the Word still carried, and still carries, power and presence.

When we are asked to say who we are, we often answer that question by saying what we do. For example, I served in the US Navy, so I would call myself a sailor. We often identify with what we do instead of who we are. Our identities and inheritance are closer than we can ever imagine. The Word of God is our balance. With every word, we receive the ability to function normally and be transplanted from our lives unto his life. The purpose is not to replace us, but to become engrafted inside of us so we can become fully functional and operational.

The Word of God reveals the true nature of humankind. We are of Adam or we are of Christ. The seed is the Word we need to be fruitful, and it can remain hidden for some time when we allow it. Our greatest gift is his Word revealed. I want to point out that, after Moses spent his time with God, the glory was so evident upon his face. Our time with God is precious in his sight. It's a time when we can just be ourselves. Nothing is hidden from God. All things are revealed in that moment of truth. All things pale in comparison to this glory.

> So God created man in his own image, in the image of God he created him; male and female he created them. (Genesis 1:27)

The face is the front part of the person's head from the forehead to the chin. It also represents the image and countenance of God and humankind. The image that we behold carries a great reward. It is also the image we portray and reflect. The face is a place of character. It is what lives inside of us that is usually reflected on the surface of the face. Looking at a person's face tells a lot about the individual. The heart of God is reflected through the face, which reveals much. God created humankind in his own image. It is truly a sobering thought to know that we are created that way.

The heart of God is reflected through his Word and through people. We were born into this world under Adam's image, but we have a great reward, and it is Jesus and his nature. His nature came at such a terrible price. His nature is never to be taken lightly. It is a high calling. The Word of God will lift you there.

We look at ourselves in a certain way and identify with that image. We can spend a lifetime building up this image. When I was younger, I covered most of my body with tattoos. It was an image that I worked at pretty hard. You can see the story of my life in outward images. Many of them I do not like, but they are a part of my outward image. They are a part of me. My relationship with God is the only thing that can make me feel regret. He has used the darker parts of my life as a place from which to propel his light.

> But the Lord said to Samuel, "Do not look on his appearance or on the height of his stature, because I have rejected him. For the Lord sees not as man sees: man looks on the outward appearance, but the Lord looks on the heart." (1 Samuel 16:7)

God intently looks on the hearts of humankind. It has taken a long time to surrender to God what was his already. We were created in his own image, and that gives him sole ownership. We like to wear masks, which requires a lot sweat and work. God's purpose in humankind is to return us back to the place of him and us. When we don the mask, we hide from the reality of the truth. The truth will cause light to shine forth out of any dark situation. I find it completely odd that the Father gives us choice when he owns it all. His creation is not robotic, but it lives and moves and has its being in each person. It may manifest in different ways, but it all comes from one source. Free will ends with a choice. One thing is for certain: God chose his original blueprint, and it is he and you.

Being born into the Adam nature certainly gives us a time we might call a reflective period during which we may try to figure out the purpose of life. The time spent figuring out who we are can be a very hectic time. Trial after trial, we test the fabric of what we know to be truth. It can also be an opportunity to stop and gaze into the mirror of God's Word.

Being born again into the Christ nature gives us the ability to change even the smallest of circumstances, altering the course of defeat to sudden victory. The more we know who God is, the more we will know about ourselves. We were created in his image. Shouldn't we take a peep at the original blueprint to have guidance for our own lives? The Word of God is many things to many people. What does it mean to you?

It takes a lot of courage to step out into the unknown, trusting that God will make it known. We get very comfortable with ourselves and the way things are. Usually when it comes to change, I drag my feet a little because I know there are risks involved with change. Change is often uncomfortable to most because we like things the way they are. But change is essential to life. Without change we become stagnant. Even though the Word of God is a sure source, change certainly can be a scary thing at first.

We carry things on the inside and are driven by raw emotions and feelings toward one another and God. This is why it must start from the inside out. We hide behind our emotions, becoming what we know and what we create from the inside. We become storehouses of information. I can remember things to this day about my childhood. The scary part is how much we can actually retain. The thought of it is mind-boggling. We could simply remain hidden for years. Most times we cater to our feelings but rarely step out on faith.

When we are driven solely by emotion, we deal with approval and disapproval. When we act out and declare our faith, we know that the guidelines of approval and disapproval have been tried through the works of Jesus Christ. God clearly defines what he approves of and disapproves of. We have planted seeds all throughout our lives that have become rooted deeply within us. The fruit of our emotions will always surface and manifest itself. The same is true with the Word of God: when planted, it will manifest.

I think it's safe to say we have all had our share of both types of behavior. When I was younger, I would lie to get approval. If there was one thing that my father hated, it was that I lied about anything. Our lies change the expression of who we are. The act of approval is officially coming into agreement with acceptance, while disapproval is the expression of an unfavorable opinion. When we come into agreement with acceptance, the approval is forged by the power of covenant. The agreement of two becomes one. The act of disapproval is just an unfavorable opinion, but it doesn't hold any truth.

> The heart is deceitful above all things, and desperately
> sick; who can understand it? (Jeremiah 17:9)

The heart is often identified as the center of each person. The heart can be the seat of emotion, but it is also where the innermost person is hidden. The heart can be sick from time to time. I surely remember times when my heart was sick. Out of the heart flow the issues of life. This can be messy when we are driven by emotions. Our emotions have us tossed about like a ship on raging sea, but the Word of God calms the storm and enables us to overcome the issues. The Word reveals the nature of the innermost man. Oftentimes when we are faced with the most difficult decisions, our emotions become revealed so we can conquer them with truth.

The act of approval is us coming into agreement with acceptance of God's Word. He never bypasses our will. It's our choice whether or not we want to reveal our innermost thoughts and intents of the heart. He sent his Word to reveal the hidden nature that was given to all humankind. Even though he is with us in every issue of life, he guides us into present truth. He guides us through every emotion offering us truth. This is why Jesus is the Word of God. He is with us in the flesh because he became flesh. He is with us in Spirit because he lives. He became our life and our death.

There is power in his Word because he became flesh and dwelled among us. He experienced everything that we would ever encounter. It is also powerful because he lives, not just for today but forever. His example fulfills both testaments. With every Word that is spoken follows power to overcome. His Word carries great authority because it experienced the Adam nature that man is born with. Jesus was tempted with all things, yet he didn't sin. On the cross he experienced death and also experienced life. He was truly the fulfillment of God in full demonstration.

> By this you know the Spirit of God: every spirit that confesses that Jesus Christ has come in the flesh is from God and every spirit that does not confess Jesus is not from God. This is the spirit of antichrist, which you have heard is coming and now is in the world already. (1 John 4:2–3)

———◆———

We have to recognize that Jesus came in the flesh to deal with sin and the nature of Adam. When a word carries great authority it unleashes life and death. It releases the testimony of his heart. A testimony is a witness borne in behalf of something. The witness is born from above, and the testimony is on behalf of his Son, Jesus, and those who are born after him. The testimony of the cross releases life and death. It releases death through the sacrifice of Jesus Christ while it tenders life to those who know God and his Son, Jesus. It is a two-edged sword that cuts down to the core of humankind.

CHAPTER SEVEN

The Door: From Death to Life

I have experienced a lot of death, but never any that was as sacrificial as the testimony of Jesus. Death is the action or fact of dying, or the end of life. Most people refer to death as not breathing, but I have been in a state of emotion in which death and darkness were imminent. When our testimony is darkness and death, we will see the manifestation of it. It seems harmless to lie for approval, but with each lie the expression changes.

> For a will takes effect only at death, since it is not
> in force as long as the one who made it is alive.
> (Hebrews 9:17)

In the case of a will there has to be a testator. A testator is a person who dies leaving a will or testament in force. The testator must clearly identify himself or herself as the maker of the will and publish it. It must also be declared and must be signed, signifying the testament that is sent forth as evidence. The Greek word for testator is *diatithemai*, which is defined as conferring, assigning, decreeing, appointing, ordaining, and making a covenant. The testament that is sent forth is absolute truth and has to be executed. The executing of the will brings the testament to force because there is power in believing and demonstrating the will. This is why it must be truth. Even the slightest lie is a lie and alters the course of following and pursuing truth. This is how Adam and Eve found themselves outside the garden. There are many words we can choose to believe, but there is one Word that is truth, and his name is Jesus.

The testator, by words, arranges and disposes of his or her own possessions and affairs. By speaking, the word goes forth to accomplish the work that was set before it, causing a perfected bond of truth. The testator sets truth in place and then demonstrates it for all to see. The force and power of the will is dependent on the testament that goes forth. When all else fails, the testament will be sure. Oftentimes we live on one side of the covenant or the other, but it's seeing and knowing the truth that sets fullness in place.

> We will not hide them from their children, but tell
> to the coming generation the glorious deeds of the
> Lord, and his might, and the wonders that he has
> done. (Psalm 78:4)

Jesus clearly was named the Word of God. I believe the Word was God in the flesh to serve as the evidence of that present truth. Jesus was not only his Word, he was also the testament that was sent forth. He was breathed forth to ease the human condition. He is the mediator between God and humankind. The Word of God is breathed inspiration to humankind. It leaves an everlasting legacy upon all those who receive it. It creates and forms the invisible. It forges the impossible.

> Jesus proclaimed, "Nevertheless, I tell you the
> truth: it is to your advantage that I go away, for if

I do not go away, the Helper will not come to you.
But if I go, I will send him to you." (John 16:7)

Jesus was crucified because he was the testament and came in great force. As horrible as it was, the cross is evidence of his great love for us. Jesus came as flesh simply to present the truth. He came by water and blood. His coming in the flesh and opening the womb as a firstborn declared him holy to the people. The Spirit testifies because it is truth. He leaves his mark on humankind, as his testimony is alive in each believer to present to others.

And when he came up out of the water, immediately
he saw the heavens being torn open and the Spirit
descending on him like a dove. (Mark 1:10)

As Jesus came out of the water, the heavens tore open and the Spirit descended on him like a dove. There is a great shift that happens here.

Jesus told John, "Let it be so now, for thus it is fitting for us to fulfill all righteousness." Then he consented. (Matthew 3:15)

Although Jesus would go through great sufferings, the Word had to pass by to be so. There is a merging of heaven and earth. The heavens tore open because Jesus is the veil into what is holy. He is the covering that protects us from all the glory of God and his brilliance. He is also the veil that is torn off to reveal a greater glory in us. He is the fullness of God and the completion of our words and work here on earth. Without him, it is impossible to pass over.

The Jewish festival Passover commemorates the exodus of the Jewish people from the bonds of slavery. God gave Moses the blueprint to pass over but had not yet appeared in the flesh to the people. To commemorate is to serve as a memorial in the fashion of a ceremony. The people were instructed to take a male lamb without spot or blemish into their household. They were also told to mark the doorposts and the lintels of their doors with the blood of the lamb. They were to roast the lamb on the fire and eat it with unleavened bread and bitter herbs—eat it with their belts fastened, their sandals on their feet, and their staffs in their hands.

He said, "It is the Lord's Passover." (Exodus 12:11)

We often identify with Jesus and the crucifixion when we identify with the blood. The blood is a sign for us and our houses. It will cause the Lord to pass over us and let no plague befall or destroy us. The blood seals and is a sign or notice for all who may enter. This blood is a sign of covenant. It represents the marking of truth. The spotless lamb must be taken inside. In those days they took the lamb inside. This would be representative of the sacrifice that they would make to God. By an act of faith, they began to build upon what was spoken by God about sealing the doorposts with blood. The people made their will be known by this simple act of faith. This was the "Passover" from this life to his life. It is simply to partake of his covenant and the power that comes from the testimony of his blood.

> The law of the Lord is perfect, reviving the soul.
> The testimony of the Lord is sure, making wise
> the simple. (Psalm 19:7)

His testimony is sure, making the wise simple. I want to paint this picture in the imagery of your mind: a perfect lamb inside an imperfect vessel sealed with the sent and returned Word of God. This Word is lying under the surface with the hope that it will be revealed. The Word was sent for us so we could refresh our souls and make this testimony simple. Jesus always is the answer. He ascended to prepare a place for us. That place is in him and it is seated and heavenly. He ascended to show us a better way. He became the pattern whereby we may know heavenly things.

The only way to escape the world is to find a better way. He didn't draw us out of the world, but he empowers us while we are here. He demonstrates a better way. He's not far away or pie in the sky; rather, he is real and proves himself to be near. He never leaves us or forsakes us. He is our escape from a pattern of this world. His Word ushers life and the presence of the holy. It creates heaven on earth and resides in the most important place it can: in each of us.

Passover is more than just a ceremony or tradition. I would never take that right-of-passage from people, but it is so much more than the exterior offers it to be. Passover is a person and the personal work of God and his Word in us. It moves us from a place of toil and sweat and from the place of pangs and birth. There is nothing greater than knowing that, as we take our journey, someone has already walked through everything we could possibly walk through. The gospel doesn't offer a life without tribulation, but it offers us a way through every trial. The gospel also provides someone to hold our hands who was not spared any temptation.

Access to the entrance comes from covering the lintel and the doorposts with blood and crossing the threshold with your feet prepared with the gospel of peace. Taking the lamb inside is a vivid metaphor for being a partaker of the Word of God. It is also symbolic of the Passover from flesh to spirit—a place where the heart is transformed and regenerated. This is where the true testimony happens. This is where the Word of God collides with the hearts of humankind. Access comes through a blemish-free and spotless Lamb. His name is Jesus.

Jesus said, "Truly, truly, I say to you, I am the door of the sheep." (John 10:7)

He clearly declared himself as the door of the sheep. To enter into the presence of God is a holy and consecrated thing. It is not only to consider ourselves as God's sheep and the door as his passage to the pasture; we can consider the door as an entrance that he has made for us into a place that is not made with human hands. He provides the way into what is holy and also becomes the sacrifice that makes it possible for us to pass over. Although this came to Moses as a shadow to host the presence of God, it was imperative that he was obedient to the call. What we are framing now will become our future. The transfiguration is a constant reminder of God's faithfulness as Moses stood there with him.

It is an amazing fact that the cross has a horizontal beam, a vertical beam, and a spiritual threshold into life. There are a few parts of the doorway that I would like to light. The lintel is the beam that runs horizontally and forms the upper part of the framework of the doorway. Although it is the top piece of the doorway, it acts as a foundation for the wall and the rest of the structure that is built upon it. The lintel carries the weight and is a reminder of our light and easy load when we trust that he has dealt with every care in our lives. He does that through his Word. He gives himself to you.

The jambs are the two sides of the door framing that run vertically. The door is secured to one of the jambs with some sort of hinge. When I look doorjambs, I am reminded of a way up or down. The Word of God came down as flesh for all humankind but also returned back from where it came. The jamb also holds the weight of the door through the hinges, making the door secure and available to open or close. The plumb of the door determines if it is truly vertical or not. When the plumb of the door isn't correct, the door doesn't open or close properly, making entrance or exit difficult and sometimes almost impossible.

The sill or the threshold of the doorway is the horizontal piece at the bottom of the structure. When the door is open, we step over the threshold to gain entrance into the dwelling. The sill also supports the framework around the door. The word *threshold* is not only used in architectural terms; it represents the magnitude or intensity that must be exceeded for a certain reaction or condition to be manifested.

> Therefore thus says the Lord God, "Behold I am the one who has laid as a foundation in Zion, a stone, a precious cornerstone, of a sure foundation. Whoever believes will not be in haste." (Isaiah 28:16)

The Word was with God and the Word was God. Understanding the mystery of enlightenment starts with the fear of the Lord. It is the beginning of wisdom. Without turning toward God, we have no other means for filling this dark void with light. The lintel is horizontal and holds and backs all the promises of God. It is the cornerstone in which the Word flows vertically, first through Jesus, and then through the foundation of apostles and prophets. The Word is carried through the blood and its testimony that gives life to the body. The weight of his inheritance is passed down through many people and many generations who desire to give birth to new life through his seed.

> Every good gift and every perfect gift is from above, coming down from the Father of lights with whom there is no variation or shadow due to change. Of his own will he brought us forth by the Word of truth, that we should be a kind of first fruits of his creatures. (James 1:17–18)

Although the lintel is the top part of the door, it acts as a foundation and carries the weight of the Word. Jesus is the cornerstone and the ground floor of faith. To come before him, you must only believe! I truly believe in this place where all words are tested through the filter of his Word. The foundation is an essential part of what structures our faith. It is the lowest load-bearing point and has underlying bases and principles. Most times we don't see what is underneath the surface. I believe that's why faith is required.

> Everyone then who hears these Words of mine and does them will be like a wise man who built his house on the rock. And the rain fell, and the floods came, and the winds blew and beat on that house, but it did not fall, because it had been founded on the rock. (Matthew 7:24–25)

Our words always have a way of being uncovered. Even though they can be hidden below the surface for a time, those words must come out. They are tested on this very foundation. It is a foundation that is sure. His Word is the simple truth. There is a nice exchange that goes on with words. We exchange our earthly language for his heavenly language. There is no communion like the one that happens when we understand and become a part of his Word in the earth. If only we could see that our lives are epistles and testimonies. He simply needs a piece of stained glass to shine through.

> For he looks at himself and goes away and at once forgets what he was like. (James 1:24)

Most times we don't even comprehend that the Lord is not limited to shining through a piece of stained glass. His light pierces the darkness, seeping into the crevices of our hearts and invading them. He fills the void of a broken and suffering flesh. There is a great transformation happening, but we look with natural eyes. We look through the eyes of Adam. At first glance, it appears to be all together, but it is broken and desperately in need. He calls us to remembrance to the grandest time of all—the time when there is nothing to hold on to but him.

When I was younger, I absolutely loved to get tattooed. I would frequently visit the shop, sometimes to get tattooed and other times just to hang out with my friend Sean. The one thing that I realize is that, no matter where you go, God will go with you. I can remember contemplating one of my tattoos. Most of the images I chose are portraits of the life I lived. I seldom have regrets because God has used the tattoos as a conversation starter, and this leads into a witness of his testimony. Where some reject us, many more will come as we learn to trust God.

My good friend Sean would say, "Your tattoos are like stained glass. Every temple has some stained glass."

This is why I have no regrets. Although some of my tattoos are downright disgusting to some, God's light knows how to shine through stained glass. Most certainly we are a temple of the Living God and subject to illumination as the heart learns to trust and let go. We are not perfect in any way, but perfected by the perfect one. He chooses all of us willingly in order to illuminate his Word and will.

The beautiful thing about stained glass is that, as light shines through, it illuminates the inside of the temple. When light shines through stained glass, a beautiful image is created on the inside of the temple as the temple is illuminated. This is why we have to let go of the flesh. The new nature of Christ and his Word reigns from within. We see beauty on the outside, but it is inside that projects the heart's intent. This happens with words and is followed by a demonstration of those very words. That's why we must choose.

He illuminates through the stained pieces of glass in your life. It is amazing that he chose to take the stains and the blemishes of humankind. The tattoos that I have on my skin will be with me while I'm in this flesh—even six months later, after my body gives its last breath. But by then I will have continued on into eternal life with something much greater. God engrafted his Word in my heart, and that itself is life and his testimony in my heart.

My dad absolutely hated my tattoos but never kept his love for me at bay, even when he was staring death in the face at a very young age. One thing I learned during that time is love never fails. It prevails and overcomes any situation or trial, even indifference. I was raised not to mark the temple and to honor God by not doing so, but my tattoos never stopped his love. It was fierce and unrelenting to him. It was part of being a man. It is honorable to carry this trait and pass it on to my children. The deeds of humankind will always be revealed through the intent of the heart. For this reason alone, no matters should be left unsaid.

I could remember when my dad was in the hospital. We all had a hard time with him having cancer at a young age. While we are there we always become aware that it could be worse. My dad made plenty of friends during his stay on the second floor. Even while facing death, he gripped life. I don't think any of us is ready to die and to put away this flesh. We are built exactly the same way, but different. We have maximum potential to meet eternal resolve. That's a gift that can never be stripped away. They can take our buildings and our Bibles, but they can't take away our hearts.

To live faith and life out loud requires trust. Every gift comes from above and comes in the fullness of his Word. It was a cold day in February when Dad left this life and entered his. I know now that Dad started life the day he uttered the name above all names, but sometimes we look through a glass dimly. On that day, a piece of my heart left me. I stood there with the pieces of my stained glass gathered in my hands, and they broke apart at my feet, or so I thought. It took me years to understand, but I believe he would have done it in moments. Just like my dad, my Father would have picked up the pieces right away and mended them, but I didn't choose him at the time.

———◆———

Today is the day of salvation—not yesterday, not tomorrow, and not next year, but today. We fight the inevitable. We try to put the pieces back together by ourselves but can't. It's the realization of the gift from above that makes the demonstration real in our lives. There is a reason that he never changes. He remains the same yesterday, today, and forever because the gift of salvation comes in the sacrifice of his flesh.

CHAPTER EIGHT

The Door is Open!

I llumination comes from this simple truth: when light shines in dark places, darkness has no other option but to be lit with the truth. While darkness is painful to erase, his blood is like a magic eraser. It makes all things new. Yielding to him takes away the sting of death and pain. The dullness of life fades, and the life of Christ is birthed and illuminated. The only thing I ever learned about death and pain is that life is better, and that, while death and pain are very real to the flesh, we have retreat and rest in Jesus.

Pieces of stained glass have to be cut and formed and assembled into the image they ultimately take on. Although the human heart is flesh and blood, it has reflective qualities. The heart can be seen by God and later by humankind. The workmanship of the heart does show. It is made manifest by the light. Stained glass, after it is cut, is rough around the edges, but the edges are healed by the lead that surrounds each piece of glass in the finished product. This analogy has stuck with me since I first heard it: the heart also can be cut deep to the core, but Jesus, the Word of God, is between the cut edges to fill, form, and frame his craftsmanship.

We know he frames the world with his Word. He fills in the cuts with himself. He sands and polishes the rough spots and makes them smooth. He frames the finished piece with a heavy and a sure frame that holds all the broken pieces together. It's in this utter place of brokenness that we grip to his glory. Although it has taken me years to recover from my past, he forgave me in a day. In a moment and in the twinkling of an eye, we change from glory to glory.

When I was wroth with God during one visit with my dad at the hospital, my dad sent me down two rooms to meet a very young couple. Just like my dad, the young man had cancer in his body. I went down to visit just to be respectful to my dad. When I arrived, the young man greeted me with a smile. His family clung to their prayers, and they were there all together. It took me years to understand why Dad had sent me down to that room. I used to think he sent me because of the life lesson he wanted me to value. Over the years I've understood that he wanted me to see that they were together, no matter what, and that in God's Word there is unity.

I am very thankful to have met this young couple; it was an honor. Sometimes we are so blind that we can't see just beyond the bridges of our noses. I have never seen them since. Just as the pattern is drawn on the glass and it is cut, so is this family in my heart. Our experiences in this life train us for the eternal equipping that soothes the heart and makes it whole. Soon after I met them, the young man passed away, but I will always remember his family and their words and his beautiful smile.

When I think of the framework God has placed around my stained glass and the blueprint that he planted inside, I stand in awe of him. It is a heavy frame of protection that he has put around the fragile parts of my stained-glass heart. Just as his hands were stretched out on the beams of that cross, his hands are stretched out around our hearts. His hands are outstretched not just for our healing but also for our entire wholeness. His hands are a safe place for our hearts. They are there to lift us up.

Many years passed before I could really feel any kind of peace about my dad's death. At the time, I was on an eight-day stretch at work and was very tired when the Lord spoke to me. He said, "I need you to go to a church meeting in Hagerstown tonight."

I simply replied, "No, Lord. I am very tired and do not want to go tonight."

He spoke again and said, "I need you to go to Hagerstown tonight. The first words you will hear will be the words you need to hear to move forward and to be healed."

As tired as I was, I left work at seven and headed to Hagerstown. The meeting started at seven, but I figured I would have time to make it for the word. As I walked in, I was greeted and then found a seat. The members of the group were finishing up worship. I remember experiencing peace as soon as I sat down and awaited the Words of God. Even though he would speak them through a man, I had peace with that.

When we find ourselves out in the pigpen and feel like a prodigal, it's hard to believe that God will speak. I am often convinced that he speaks in that state or frame of mind when things are utterly broken and it seems they cannot ever be repaired. Being honest, that is where I was with my dad's death. I had run as far as I could and spent what I had to do it. I was in the proverbial pigpen of life, but God spoke. No matter how far we run, he will be there to meet us.

We have plenty of time to think when we are in the pen. It seems like a reprisal of all our past memories. Something was different that night as I sat there and awaited the Word. I believe the difference in that night and any other night was that I wanted to hear, I wanted change, I wanted to feel better, and above all, I wanted to be free. Often we see ourselves as dirty and undeserving, but the Word of God shakes that mindset. It levels the playing field, making the paths straight again. He makes all things new. Every thought, every memory, and every feeling is held captive to his Word. It seemed as a sat there, I could feel the expectation building.

As the spirit of the people began to wind down from worship

the speaker arose and started working the crowd. Even though we might be in a room full of people, with God we feel as if we are alone with him. His attention is undivided and totally on each of us. It was years of preparation before that one moment. Even as the crowd pressed in for more, everything around me silenced. The whole room was buzzing, but it felt still and peaceful. In that moment and a twinkling of an eye all things were about to change and be new.

> And Samuel said, "Has the Lord as great delight in burnt offerings and sacrifices, as in obeying the voice of the Lord? Behold, to obey is better than sacrifice, and to listen than the fat of the rams." (1 Samuel 15:22)

Listening to the Lord at the appointed time will yield a great harvest, not only in our lives but in those around us. Our obedience to his voice and call is our humble sacrifice to him. It is a gift from above. It's only fitting to give what we have been given. It's his Word—nothing more, nothing less—that brings a new nature with the testimony and power to overcome. We can stand there with all the broken pieces of our stained glass, or we can choose to give them to him.

As the speaker stood, he grabbed the microphone and began to pace up and down in front of the crowd. Members of the audience could see the anticipation on his face as well. The Word God gave him to release was weighted with glory and would change my life the moment it was spoken. What I mean by weighted in glory is that it was powerful yet lifting. I knew God could ease the human condition in just a moment, but it takes obedience and submission to speak and give God what is his and his alone. We must give our hearts.

The weight of his glory comes in the revelation and knowledge of his suffering for us. In every one of your moments and breaths he has not forsaken us. In every one of our needs he presents himself anew and fresh. It is weighted glory because all sin was poured upon him, and he doesn't share his glory with any man. Although we are a part of the fellowship of his sufferings, it is a knowledge and revelation of what he's accomplished for us. He came first for all things then freely gives the revelation as a testimony to overcome.

The speaker spoke these four words: "The door is open."

At these four words my world was melted. All the years of running and hiding seemed very distant to the reality of what I was seeing. The splendor of a king and his kingdom unfolded before my eyes. It was as if the scales were rolled away from my eyes. The Word of God opens up a very real reality. It is multifaceted like a gem, but it is whole. At one glance we see many promises accomplished. There is so much splendor as we gaze at him.

> Where there is no prophetic vision the people cast
> off restraint, but blessed is he who keeps the law.
> (Proverbs 29:18)

I have realized that the Word of God changes the heart and allows room for the vision to come to pass. It places a great hope from within. Without the Word, our vision is cast off and despondent. He is our hope and future. We have a dream and a vision for our own future, but without the Word of God, the pieces seem separate. The Word gives us hope and sharpens our courage. It takes our dream and vision and makes it a reality. We see the whole picture.

When I heard those words—"The door is open!"—Wow! The door flung wide open, and there was nothing left to do but enter. God's presence is so inviting. It lacks nothing and is not shortened by our limitations or expectations. He shatters the limits with lively hope in an unseemly situation. I walked in as a result of simple obedience, fighting all the way there, and despite that, he blessed it all. The Word makes way where our way seems nearly impossible to pass. He lifts us to a place where we can pass, where all the pieces come together and the image becomes clear.

Our hearts can be clouded by fear, but the Word of God makes the image known before darkness. He shrouds us with his glory when we come to a place of understanding his sufferings. It would seem that all hope would be lost, but his Word rises to the occasion perfectly and at the right time. It is fitting that the only place the Word of God belongs is in our hearts, and we are temples of a living God. He decides to inhabit us. Because our hearts are where the Word is, he not only is lifted, but he lifts us too. He brings us to a place of understanding through his Word.

At his Word, the vision comes to pass, but we must have heart to endure the small affliction that is on our lives. Knowing him and the work he accomplished makes it small. I could never confess that when I didn't know him, and still to this day I simply have to let go when things get rough. I simply put one foot in front of the other and trust him even when I can't see the next step. Faith requires us to step into unknown areas. It requires us to trust him even when a situation doesn't look or feel right. We find ourselves in a place where we can bear fruit, and that fruit takes time.

CHAPTER NINE

His Word Realized

Jesus said, "To you it has been given to know the secrets of the Kingdom of God, but for others in parables, so that seeing they may not see, and hearing they may not understand."

—Luke 8:10

The Word of God is the seed that enables the fruit of God to take root in our lives. At first, we read the scriptures, and we have very limited understanding of them. We are consumed by the affliction or trial, and often we pray out of despair because there is nowhere to turn. The Word of God is a parable to us until we understand that it is seed. When we know it is seed, we must have faith to frame the unknown. Then we must have patience and wait upon that seed to become fruit in our lives. After the seed is planted, the application of faith is required before we can bring forth and harvest the fruit. He gives us his Word, but we must be the stewards of it.

> Many are the afflictions of the righteous, but the Lord delivers him out of them all. (Psalm 34:19)

We are definitely byproducts of our words. That is why it is important to have knowledge of God's Word. It delivers us from every one of our afflictions. It leads us out of every one of our problems. Having a general knowledge is one thing. There are many who can recite the Bible verse by verse and still not have any real demonstration in their lives because they do not fully surrender. Not to pick, but many have great knowledge of the Word but don't recognize the Word. I was one of them until he awakened me with his Word.

Before knowing God, I lived a darkened life! I seemed like a good person to most people, but I certainly wasn't living by the Word of God. When I got into trouble I would pray, but I had little understanding. These prayers were cries when I needed him, but when I didn't need him, I didn't have time for him. I know now that his heart cries out for us moment by moment. He doesn't relent. He doesn't give up as we do sometimes when the answer isn't what we want to hear. I know now that serving him has to be a wholehearted endeavor. It's not perfect, but perfected.

I am thankful, though, for the many prayers that were prayed on my behalf when I labeled myself as a drunken sailor. That yoke carried a lot of weight and self-afflicted troubles. The labels of this world pale in comparison to the glory that awaits us now and even in this present life. I don't look at sharing these stories to compete over how much worse I could have been than the next person; rather, I share because I deeply believe that I wouldn't want anyone to walk in these shoes. I couldn't even walk in them myself. I had to be relieved of those shoes and be fitted with the gospel of peace.

I once heard a man say, "Boy, you wouldn't want to walk in my shoes."

I looked at him and said, "Yes. I couldn't even walk in my own! Why would I want to walk in yours?"

The troubles and afflictions in this world are multiplied by the words and labels we decide to carry. God's Word is the yoke that is placed upon our hearts. It governs the speed of how life comes at us. It is a significant understanding when we realize the difference between how much God loves us and that he is love. Loving someone is starkly different from becoming love forever. Above all, he is love. His Word is his love letter to you. When you know who he is, you are righteous. You become his likeness. The labels will fall away.

I have never been a fan of struggling and being afflicted, but I have learned one thing from it all: the Word of God is far superior to any name or anything I could ever hope or dream of. It was through my struggles that I learned to depend on the Word of God and not myself. My heart's desire is that you will retire from the school of hard knocks and know that his Word is light and easy. Sometimes it takes hardship to break through the harder shell of the heart. I am very sympathetic to those who go through affliction. The only thing I learned from affliction is that the Word of God is so much better.

> And the Lord said to her, "Two nations are in your womb, and two peoples from within you shall be divided. The one people shall be stronger than the other and the older shall serve the younger." (Genesis 25:23)

I can really identify with Jacob's story because we can do everything wrong, but in one day it can all change. The name Jacob in the Hebrew language means to supplant. To supplant is to take the place of another through force or to replace one thing by another. The main point that I want to convey is that there are two very different natures of humankind. One is taken by force while the other is just given. Certainly humankind is capable of the same thing when we are undecided.

Many times in my life I have been faced with the most difficult decisions. These decisions have paved the way for the outcome of my life. God and his nature are ever so real. The tangible presence of God and the reality of his Word can change things in one day. The heart must submit to it in order for the true nature to manifest. When I look at humankind, I see the two natures. There is an utter darkness to contend with, but there is also the light. The words of our mouths reveal the true nature that is deeply inside. It has been in these difficult times that he has drawn me to his Word. He ever lives to make covenant with us. In hard times, we must seek him. Real results require change.

These patterns are evident all throughout the Bible. God always communicates his Word with humankind, but we have to be able to hear his voice. Seeking after him allows opportunity for the Word of God to present itself. I believe he is always present with us, but we have to slow down our speech to be able to hear. His Word is not only our pattern, but it is what puts life together for us. He demonstrates that he is life and the abundance of it.

The words that we value in our hearts manifest. If we speak them, they can and will come into being whether they are good or bad. When you give power to them, they will manifest. I had an awful experience one time, but I learned that evil does exist and that it is right outside the door waiting to creep in. In reality, what we speak will become our truth. This is why the Word of God was sent down. It gives us a way out.

They say that image can be everything. What we speak and believe we will surely become. I want to share this story with you. It is about the time I learned that evil actually exists. Before that time, I believed that we could speak with no consequences. I believed that our own words could easily be erased. But I was wrong. It was eleven in the morning, and my friends and I were drinking already and having a good time. Unaware, I drank a cup of beer that was laced with drugs. Before long I was hallucinating and getting very sick. Most people would say that what I saw was all in my imagination, but I beg to differ.

I asked my friends to take me home because I had to lie down for a while. Before we left, I went into the bathroom to wash my face. I stared in the mirror for a moment and realized that there was an aura of darkness around me. It was attached to my midsection, and it hovered over my head. My first thought was, "This isn't real!" I leaned down to splash water on my face, and when I looked up again, I saw the darkness very clearly—and I knew what it was. I had chosen to live this way, and a great darkness had manifested through my unbelief.

It enraged me. I knew I had heard the voice of God when I was sixteen. I asked, "How could he allow this!"

I didn't want to take any responsibility for any of my actions. I was so furious at my reflection that I smashed my face into the mirror, shattering it into pieces. Large pieces of glass fell to the floor at my feet, and small shards of glass dusted my face. My friends had to pay for the mirror so the police wouldn't be called. They took me home to sleep it off, but the experience stuck with me for a long while.

Now I would never question God's motive or plan, but then I questioned everything. I was in the dark for many years after that happened, but one day as I sought him, I got my answer. It happened while I was in prayer one morning. I was left speechless after he spoke. I hadn't expected that to happen, and I wasn't even aware of it when it did happen. His Word has an amazing way of settling things that we struggle with. It brings an end to a means.

He spoke and said, "I made humankind in my likeness and image. When you desired to destroy my image, I covered your face with my hand."

Usually when a person smashes his or her face into a mirror there would certainly be some facial damage, especially if there was a brick wall behind the mirror, as there was behind the mirror I "attacked"! Yet I wasn't cut, bruised, or damaged in any way whatsoever. Whenever I do decide to share the story, most people are taken aback, but I tell them that I believe he truly watched over me. I couldn't say in words how grateful I am. If I spent the rest of my life helping others, it wouldn't even come close to repaying him for the tender mercies that have been afforded me.

He is a very merciful God, and I was very aware of it after that day. He brought me back to the place in my heart where I was when he first spoke to me about the call. Even though we become more like him daily through the Word of God, our dependency on the relationship should be greater. The closer we get to him the more transparent we should be. Surely, you will know he is in this place.

Abraham, Isaac, and Jacob were the patriarchs of the origins of the Jewish people but they learned by God the same way we do. They were all given the promise of the seed in the earth. Contending for God's seed in this realm could be the greatest endeavor we will ever face. We as a people have to overcome our earthly tabernacles, letting them be dissolved by the glory and the presence of his Word. Even though we live our lives in this flesh, we are not of the flesh. We will eventually stand before God, and the Word of God will be our new habitation. We are new creatures in Christ because he is the Word and is never far from us.

Abraham was named by God as the father of many nations, and his seed would multiply upon the earth. The most important thing that we could ever do is wait on the promise. Abraham and Sarai were promised seed but began to get older in age while not seeing that seed come to pass. They took matters into their own hands. Sarai wanted family so badly she decided to have it any way she could have it. When God speaks to us, he gives us precise direction, and provides the answer. He isn't a by-product of our decisions; rather, he *is* the solution. We simply have these two choices: we can try to work this thing out ourselves, or we can believe God for his Word.

In my situation, I knew I heard the call, and I would like to think that I had a lot to do with it. The only thing I had to do was believe. My heart wanted to say yes, but everything from within was screaming no. I wanted to do it myself.

He was waiting on me to say, "I let go, and I will just believe you."

Never grow weary when it comes to the seed. What he has

spoken will surely come to pass if you simply believe. My family of believers prayed and believed for me. They never gave up or believed what they were seeing out of my life. They just prayed and believed God's Word. I am thankful for the seed that was planted. It framed the path for better things in my life.

We can see through Abraham's choice that it was passed down through his generations. We can also see that, when he believed, it did the same as well. Believing unlocks the mysteries of heaven. It is in the cracks of our lives that we will find God. I believe he longs to intercede for us in those cracks of our hearts simply to fill them and make us whole. It was in these cracks that I really began to know God and trust him. I found that, no matter what it was that was bothering me, he was there and available. He is a beautiful servant and at the same time a majestic king.

> You have a mighty arm; strong is your hand, high
> your right hand. (Psalm 89:13)

He surely came down as flesh and surely rose again to power at the right hand of God. In his right hand is the power to bless with you with his seed.

The scriptures are predominately clear about his right hand. When his right hand is extended, all the attributes of God are demonstrated. It is all throughout scriptures. If you have ever praised God with your hands, you might recall that your hands are often stretched forth just as his hands are toward you. They are open to those who believe, and there are pleasures forevermore to experience.

Also in the stretching of the right hand comes power and authority. He exercises his kingdom in the stretching forth of his right hand. He executes his judgments and decrees. He sends his Word this way. He not only proves that he is the King of Kings, he also demonstrates the Word by becoming a servant to all men. His Word is sent from the throne to show us who he really is. It is through the sacrifice of Jesus that we begin to understand this revelation of truth.

Queen Esther could identify with this. She was burdened by the sentence that was levied upon her people. She had to press into the innermost part of the king's court to receive the very words that would free her people. She didn't go to the king exalting herself; rather, she went to plea for the people and their freedom. She stood in the king's court waiting for him to stretch forth his scepter. As soon as he did, she placed her hand upon it and made her request be known to the king. He then answered her with great favor.

We can learn so much from Esther. Sometimes the burden we carry is so great that it consumes us. We have to make our request known before the king. If it hadn't been for this mercy, I surely would have been swallowed up by all my shoulders could carry. We don't have to beg or barter for God's blessing, but we have to humble ourselves and learn how to stand in the king's court and await his voice.

When we learn to approach him in humility, we are gifted with boldness. The promises of God are given, but we have to walk them out. I have found that with his seed comes all the supply we will ever need. It is the heart of humankind that God looks upon. When our motives are right for the blessing, he extends his hand and pours out the blessing. It is the time we spend waiting in the courts that prepares our hearts for this outpouring. It is absolutely essential to have this time.

———◆———

The Word of God is already spoken and declared over us. We just have to receive it. It is in this that we learn the right things to do. In my eyes I have done nothing worthy of this blessing, but it doesn't negate that very truth of the promise of life. There will always be a portion that is fact. It is a fact that I came up short in pleasing God for a long time, but the truth trumps facts. The truth is eternal and real. It is the truth that sets this love in action and secures our place in his courts.

CHAPTER TEN

The Ladder over the Impassible

Jacob left Beersheba and went toward Haran. And he came to a certain place and stayed there that night, because the sun had set. Taking one of the stones of the place, he put it under his head and lay down in that place to sleep. And he dreamed, and behold, there was a ladder set up on the earth, and the top of it reached to heaven. And behold, the angels of God were ascending and descending on it! And behold, the Lord stood above it and said, "I am the Lord, the God of Abraham your father and the God of Isaac. The land on which you lie I will give to you and to your offspring. Your offspring shall be like the dust of the earth, and you shall spread abroad to the west and to the east and to the north and to the south, and in you and your offspring shall all the families of the earth be blessed. Behold, I am with you and will keep you wherever you go, and will bring you

> back to this land. For I will not leave you until I
> have done what I have promised you." Then Jacob
> awoke from his sleep and said, "Surely the Lord is
> in this place, and I did not know it."
>
> —*Genesis 28:10–16*

Jacob placed his head upon a stone and lay there to rest. It is believed that he was in a place called Bethel. Bethel is defined as a holy place or a hallowed place. It is a place of consecration and sanctification. It was there that Jacob dreamed and saw the ladder set up on the earth reaching into the heavens. This holds great significance concerning our position before God and his response to us. I wouldn't see a stone as a comfortable place to rest my head. I am not sure that in those days stones were used to rest on, but the deeper spiritual significance is that it's a solid place. It's a place of security and a safe haven for the weary who need rest from their labors.

The stone is also symbolic of a place of stepping up or stumbling. The stone is solid and rigid. It is a place on which we can build, and it will be secure from anything that comes against it. The stone can also be a great place of offense and stumbling. I find it deeply remarkable that, even before the law was given to Moses, Jacob awoke from sleep and realized he was in the house of God. He rose up and took the stone he had used for a pillow and set it up for a pillar and then poured oil upon it. He offered his stone in exchange for something greater.

> And he said to him, "Truly, Truly, I say to you,
> you will see heaven opened, and the angels of God
> ascending and descending on the Son of Man."
> (John 1:51)

While Jacob was asleep, he saw a ladder that was set up on earth. It reached the heavens. The angels of God ascended and descended upon it. The Lord stood above it as he decreed his will over Jacob.

There is a transfer of wealth when we are able to comprehend and understand what God accomplished through Christ on the cross. The Word of God is the ladder over the impassible and impossible. The Word was sent, and it accomplished what it was sent to do. Its purpose was to invade earth with God's presence and to make way for humankind to have all that heaven provides.

When I was a child, I would look at the sky and think that heaven was up there somewhere. To me the clouds seemed harmless enough, and still to this day, I do not dispute our going up. Today, I know for a fact that heaven is very real place.

Once again Jesus said, "Truly, Truly, you will see the heavens opened and the angels of God ascending and descending on the Son of Man."

Have you ever wondered why Jesus always saw and did what his Father asked of him?

I have often pondered why this transformation must happen in the heart and nowhere else. I have had my stuff together at times in my life, but there have been other times when it seemed impossible for me to be together. The heart of man is the place where God works. The Word was with God, and the Word was God and it became flesh and dwelt among us. The transformation happens in the heart. As Jacob did, we must lay our heads on the rock. After the vision rises up, we must pour oil on the rock and declare it to be our pillar. It is just not the vision; it becomes reality when we make this place our place of rest.

The Word of God breathes life into the vision. I have had many dreams in my life, but none so successful as the ones that have come to pass by his Word. All good gifts come from above. They are sent and descend down from heaven. They become the threshold that we must have faith to cross. Also they become the ground floor removing the yoke of bondage and releasing the exact Word and the precise moment. Then it ascends, accomplishing what it was sent for and returning back to witness of the work. The work of God will always be portrayed by his Word.

Jacob saw the Lord at the top of the ladder. God is the lintel.

He holds the weight of the wall. His love goes further than the heavens, and his faithfulness goes further than the skies. The knowledge of his glory fills the earth. The thing that is simply amazing is that the ladder was set up on the earth and reached the heavens. This is to denote that his Word and work always come from above. It doesn't return empty, and always accomplishes what it was sent to do. It makes a way into heaven through the access of the door. The door is Jesus!

Are they not all ministering spirits sent out to serve for the sake of those who are to inherit salvation? (Hebrews 1:14)

Jesus told his disciples that they would see angels of God ascending and descending on the Son of Man.

God was the Word that came to the earth in the flesh of his Son, Jesus. Jesus became the ladder we could use to cross the chasm of certain death and to not only to escape hell but to have life like none other. He came as an example to you and me. There is no better way to come than by his Word. It started with Jesus and was passed to many saints who would hold dear to the Word and inherit salvation. With each revelation we receive comes the inevitability of his Word, but it comes only if we bow our hearts down for the understanding we need to move forward.

If we ever want to move with effectiveness, we have to be opened by his Word. We can be sent out to those in need only if we are willing to bare all to him. Just as Jesus was sent out into the earth, he sends us as a testimony to all who would see, hear, and believe. There will be many who withstand his testimony in you, but many more who will receive. What comes down will surely rise up. It rises up in all who will believe, but most importantly it returns back to the throne not void, and it accomplished what it was sent to do. It gives life back!

The rising of our faith alleviates the weight of our lives. It propels us across the threshold. If we gaze hard enough into stained glass of our lives, we will be able to comprehend his goodness in any situation. You will see that he is above all, holding up the weight. His Word will pick up the pieces of that shattered glass, and it will form a new image. It is alive and moving, coming down from the throne of grace and returning as a testimony that overcomes. The Word of God makes a way across the threshold between your lives and his. My life is not my own, but it is his.

A few years before my dad had lung cancer, he had a vision of being in a large field with the Lord. The Lord told him, "I will receive you soon. Go and prepare your house."

One day as I was sitting with my dad, he told me his story of experiencing heaven. He described it as the most beautiful thing he had ever set eyes upon. He talked about the grass, warm winds, and the clouds, and the overwhelming peace that resided there. A river ran through where he stood. My dad was always visual and could describe things that he saw to a T, and I believed him because he never lied to us. It was very weird to me because, as kids, we never went to church that much, but he believed.

When he was a young teenager, his legs were bent behind his back while he was playing football. This damaged his spinal column, and he spent a lot of time in the hospital dealing with paralysis. They were afraid that he would not walk again. While he was in the hospital, people prayed for him. The doctors operated on his back as a last resort at the request of the family. The doctors didn't guarantee anything at all with the surgery, and everyone prepared for the worst. But God answered, and my dad walked again. God demonstrated his love toward my dad, and he received it. As a young boy myself, I would see the scar on his back and often ask about it. He would tell me the story one more time.

I want to take you back now to my crossing of that threshold. Again, as I stated earlier, I heard the words, "The door is open."

The preacher proclaimed it. Immediately I could see the grass as it swayed and touched the tips of my fingers. Everything was magnified in color, and the warm breeze ushered peace. There was a river there that had crystal-clear water in it. When I looked at it I saw a young man sitting there with his feet in the river. He was praising God. I asked the Lord, "Who is that man?"

He said, "That is your dad!"

At this point, I wanted to run to him and hug him. I shouted his name, but he kept praising God. I then realized that Dad was in way better hands. The tears began to stream down my face because I was overwhelmed by peace and presence. I felt lighter because the burden of Dad's death had been lifted. Death is a heavy weight that many people carry. Before this experience, I blamed God and myself, but after this all I could do was love God and be thankful for the gift he shared with my dad and me. His gift was eternal life.

God reconciled everything in that one moment. A few years later, when I was in another meeting and thought myself completely healed of my dad's passing, the Lord showed up in a mighty way. In a vision, I saw Jesus with my dad. Dad looked at me and said, "Everything is all right between you and me."

It was in that moment that my reality was shattered by the truth. I had never felt so free in all my life. I get teary at the thought of that moment. That was the moment when it dawned on me that I was free from my dad's death, but I also realized something greater. I knew that everything was all right between God and me.

A few weeks later, God sent a healing minister my way. The minister worked his way over to me. He looked at me, and then he embraced me in a fatherly hug. He then spoke and said, "God wants you to know that everything is all right between you and him." All I could do was melt in the minister's arms and cry.

———◆———

I have learned over the years that God yearns to have covenant with his people. He doesn't want part of our hearts; he wants our entire hearts. He doesn't want to visit; he wants to dwell in our hearts. He wants to be with us when we wake, when we sleep, even when we take our next breath. He wants to be in every facet of our lives. His Word is the blueprint for the way we are to operate in his covenant.

CHAPTER ELEVEN

Covenant Equals Relationship

A covenant relationship begins when two become one. It is a hard thing to take two totally opposite people and make them one. Relationships can be very messy, and oftentimes they become broken. To be honest, I was at the end of my rope when I met the woman God sent to be my wife. God has a great sense of humor. When I met the love of this life for the first time, I was in the midst of a web of lies, and he sent a very truthful women. To this day we both laugh about it.

The truth has a way of shattering all lies. We simply must embrace the truth. When we live in lies, we deny ourselves the opportunity to embrace our true destiny. The truth sets us free. It has a way of revealing all darkness. The purpose of covenant is to learn how to be faithful. It is the same in marriage. As a husband, it is my desire to release the best of who I am to my wife. First, I am faithful, and I am thankful to God for the blessing of having a true relationship. Second, I love my wife as Christ loved his church.

I am truly in love with my wife. She is my best friend and the rose upon my arm. My wife's name is Jenny. We shared eight years together before we decided to be married. I would have married her right away, but she wasn't ready. She was always committed, and she honored me the best she knew how, and I did the same for her. It wasn't too long before we began our family. It happened really fast, and we were on our way to a happy life. A happy life is always how we start. It is what we envision for ourselves, but relationships have their share of troubles. It is by overcoming those troubles together that the relationship becomes worthwhile.

Intertwining two hearts and making them one happens through life experiences. When dealing with the issues of man and wife, we find there are some very noticeable differences between the two. Usually when entering a relationship, we understand each other only enough to just scratch the surface of the other's heart. It takes years to understand each other and to know what is pleasing to one another and in the sight of the Lord. God looks upon the heart of each person and weighs the intent of it toward him and then toward the person's partner.

Family is the fruit of the relationship. It is a great honor to have a wife and children who have known the presence of God to be real. The heart's intent is different in the life of each member of my family. We all have real struggles. We realize that we all feel different, but God has put us together for one reason or another. The fruit of the relationship comes when we truly know how to commune with God and then with each other. I find greater resolve in sharing our feelings with each other. It is finding time for one another that multiplies the blessing on our lives.

For our first eight years together, we were not married. Truly not understanding God's covenant for man and woman being one causes so many of life's issues. When we don't honor God in our relationships, we remove the possibility of so many blessings. It was never God's intent for man and wife to live outside of covenant. Marriage is the earthly way we learn to become one. He teaches us through basic yet true covenantal promises.

I do believe that, through all the stumbling, God is there,

right in the midst of the union. After about eight years, both of us were about finished with one another. We had exhausted every ounce of our strength toward one another. There wasn't another tear left, or so we thought. I didn't know what to do, so I ran. This time, though, I ran straight to God. Looking back at the situation, I don't regret my decision, but sudden change brings forth some feelings that were under the surface.

After being together for eight years and having two kids, we thought we should know about intimacy. Instead, we found ourselves trying to save our relationship with counseling. I was newly born again at the time. It was really weird for my wife to see her tattooed bad boy turn to the Lord. Her response was, "I didn't get together with a preacher."

In my eyes, I didn't see anything wrong with what I was doing. I was going to church every day the doors opened. It was a full-time thing for me. What I wasn't seeing was that I was neglecting my first ministry, my family. There is nothing wrong with going to church. I believe it's a great place to be, and we must never forsake it, but we must make time for those in our family.

I went to church one night after work because I was all out of solutions with my wife. I knew deeply in my heart that something had to change between us. The church had planned to have all the young men give their testimony that night. As the young men spoke, I listened very intently for my answer. The last speaker of the house got up. He asked, "Is there anyone here who needs help from God tonight?" He was looking for an answer, so he kept asking. He asked several times, and each time he asked, I felt more conviction in my heart. Soon I began to weep.

An older man looked over and said, "It's you who needs help."

We look at conviction as a confrontation into our own personal space. It is a place where the heart can be softened or calloused. His Word will challenge the way we think and ponder in our hearts. God will always allow us the chance to choose even when he knows the answer. He sent Moses to Pharaoh, but already knew how he would answer. He already knew the answer in my case, but I had to choose. I could keep going down the same road, or I could try something different. One thing I knew for sure was this: my family was at stake regarding my decision.

When we go to church, we hear all about the freedom that God provides through his Son, Jesus. Although we hear about it, this is something we have to experience full on. Faith comes by hearing the Word of God. It takes up residence in us. It is life to us. Not only do we hear, we also know if it's real or not. It's more than emotion or feeling, but it becomes truth and the answer we need.

The Word draws our hearts to the forefront. I stood up and began to make my way to the front. I felt as if I had a ton of bricks on my back. The further I walked, the heavier my burden felt. I fell to my knees because I couldn't take another step. As I surrendered, I knew everything that I had heard was so real. I could hear everyone rushing toward me, but my focus was on God. In our moment of surrendering nothing else matters but God and us. In such moments, each of us feels as if we are the only one in the room. His attention is all on us. There is nothing like the presence of God and his Word—nothing.

God spoke and said, "If you want her, you have to stop having her."

I thought to myself for a minute. I could hear all the prayers around me, but the voices seemed to dim as his voice grew louder. He spoke again, "If you want her, you have to stop having her."

It took a while for me to get up off the floor, and I needed help to get to my feet. I heard so many voices around me, but the one voice seemed so clear. When a church service ends, we go back to our lives, but church never ends. He is in our very innermost being. We just have to let go and yield to the heart's cry he has placed upon us. We know because suddenly we will feel as if a weight has been lifted. This is how I know I've heard. The closer I get, the lighter I feel.

God is truth. The truth is revealed through the revelation of his Son, Jesus Christ. His covenant requires a pure heart. The sins of man are purged by the tender of his sacrifice. There is not one day that goes by that I have been perfect, but yet we are perfected. We are that way because he made a way for you and me. This is the reason I had to stop having her. He doesn't just stop at words, but demonstrates his power and authority in us. There is transformation that happens when truth dwells with us and from within. It changes the way we look at things. It turns us around.

The demonstration of his Word and works comes with resistance. A few hours later, after church, I went home after making the commitment to God, and I followed through. I told my wife what had happened, and she got really upset and called me crazy. I was very serious about what had happened, so I stopped having her. It came at a price at first, but I will never regret the day I made that decision. It changed the way I looked at my wife. We became so much more after that. I couldn't imagine a day without her in my life. She is truly the rose on my arm. A few months later, we were blessed and were able to have a beautiful wedding day.

When we wed, the one we love it is just the start of the relationship. Although my wife and I lived together and had children, it was important to us to honor God and his covenant. If we give him a little, we find that we can never out-give him. He will pour out blessings through the relationship. One blessing he has poured out upon us is the ability to not have the last word. Our words will always precede actions. If we speak of our relationship as blessed and honor the covenant set before you, God will bless it.

With covenant, troubles will come, but God will deliver us out of every situation when we know how to honor. We must learn to trust God. No relationship is perfect, so we have to depend on him to make it as good as it can be. By no means are my wife and I in a perfect relationship, but we honor each other. We honor each other in our messes, in our trials, in our failures, and in our successes. Covenant becomes perfected when we bond with his Word and honor our commitments and words that we made to each other. This is where truth is demonstrated and displayed in covenant.

The fruit of our love is witnessed by God in covenant relationship. It is sealed by his Word. Honoring God and his Word will bestow honor upon us and everyone who is under the blessing. God bestows his blessings backed with his Word. The fruit of his Word is made manifest in the union and multiplies down through the generations. I know that the mandate that my wife and I chose will be passed down through the generations. It has become our testimony and will be available for our children.

Relationships become perfected when we call those things into existence that do not exist. We have to practice at this. Sharing our faith with one another will summon the words that need to be spoken. In his eyes my wife is beautiful and bold, truthful and honoring. She is a real prize. He demonstrates his Word at her love and honor toward me. The relationship becomes mutual when we return those words back to the sender. It is honoring to God when the words of our mouths are effectual and full of love. It sets the scene for greater things.

When we enter in covenant relationship, our words become his words. We learn to speak his language toward one another. We walk it out with one another. Our relationship speaks great volumes to those who observe it. Not only do we learn in the process, but also we display his love for us through covenant. We learn to let go of our words and choose his Word. Over the years, our words and demonstration of love have grown into a blossoming bush. It reminds me of the butterfly bushes we planted outside the house. We planted them at the same time, yet they are different. They bloom at different times, but we still get the same enjoyment from both.

The individual may differ, but the relationship blooms from the love that is sown into it. It makes two into one. His Word becomes the seed that eventually will be the fruit. My wife and I didn't start out with a great relationship. We just worked at it day by day. We practiced what we preached. We live life together even when it is undesirable and messy. On some days the weight of the world seems unbearable, but we always have each other and God.

I would like to share another story with you that is very dear to my heart. One morning while I was in prayer, I heard a word that seemed impossible to bear again. The Lord spoke, "I will gladly receive her soon."

I asked, "Who will you receive?"

He replied, "My daughter, Sharon."

Sharon is my mother-in-law. At first, I dismissed those words because she was still young. I didn't believe it. She was very nurturing to her family and was always there for us. Because of my upbringing, I was used to taking care of our own. My mother-in-law and I didn't see eye to eye on the raising of my children, but there was always love there. I know deeply that she cared about all of us and had deep admiration. She was and always will be a part of our lives.

Shortly after the Lord spoke to me, she was diagnosed with breast cancer, and we were all devastated at the news. It pained me to see that look on my wife's face. It was all too familiar. I knew I was free. It just hurt to see her that way. After all those years of gripping onto Dad's death and realizing that there was freedom from that, I knew we would have to walk this out together. My wife had been right by my side during all of the years when I walked through my own process. I knew in my heart of hearts that, no matter how ugly it got, I wouldn't leave her side. That was the least I could do.

The relationship my mother-in-law had with my wife and children was unbreakable. She loved them to pieces. My wife would do anything for her mom. She filled in whenever her mom needed her. She didn't run, but dug in and got ready for battle. She was truly there for her mom. It was truly admirable. I knew what she was going through to a point, but I believe each individual acts different according to what he or she believes. My wife was doing what she could.

Sharon was a believer and was certain that she would be healed of the cancer. When we are faced with the possibility of death, fear kicks in. The only thing we can do is turn to his Word and pray. We draw close to what we know to be truth. I have respect for the gift of those who practice medicine, and I am thankful for it. In times of uncertainty we need to draw closer to the Lord because he is our answer. So we prayed and believed for the miracle to happen.

The diagnosis can become our reality if we allow it to be. The facts have to be stated, but there is a deeper truth that becomes a reality in our lives. We are not of our own; rather, we are his. Most times we are not ready for someone to leave. Death is an enemy and is only overcome by the blood of Jesus and his testimony. His blood and testimony form a deep and personal bond between him and the believer. It is a covenant relationship and the sealing of our faith in him. It is our very covering.

We are always close to those we pray with. Jesus and his ministry was always among the people. He was always with them. We have to be with those whom we believe for. During this time, my wife believed her mom would be healed. Those words that I had heard rang in my ear, but I stood with Sharon and my wife on what we believed to be true. Sharon's cancer went into remission a few months later, and she was back on track to being the person she'd been before she became ill.

When we are faced with these things, we can feel doubt in our spirits. We must never bow down to the circumstances even though they can be so real. We must always be ready and available to speak truth. Words like *cancer* can change the image that we were born to display if we allow them to. It is not ours to take, but was bore on the cross by Jesus. Words can take over our identities if we take ownership of them. We lay claim to our words. It warms my heart that my mother-in-law always contended for her wholeness.

In most families there are differences that need to be reconciled. Forgiveness has to be an essential part of the relationship. Relationships need forgiveness in order to heal. Forgiveness will flow at the release of God's Word. When we repent and forgive, the order of things is restored. Forgiveness causes the rebuilding and restoration process to begin. Forgiveness is the first word that should be listed in our restoration plan. It will liberate the captive. Usually forgiveness starts with us.

During this time of remission things got back to normal with my mother-in-law. When we don't see eye to eye with someone, there is always a possibility for issues. Our hearts flow out the issues of life. Forgiveness is absolutely necessary to be free. We don't have to be right all the time. We just have to be able to stand in truth. There cannot be one stone that is left unturned. It is our responsibility to forgive to the measure we were forgiven, and we must trust God for the rest. He will meet the need every time when it comes to forgiveness.

Being unforgiving will set up a foothold in all your situations. An unforgiving heart causes pain and hurt. One of the most hurtful things that could ever happen is not receiving that forgiveness. When we don't forgive, our voices are silent. People won't hear us if we have hurt them. The stumbling block is that we are not quick to forgive. To build upon the relationship, we must forgive one another. It's the way of the Lord and the way we will become free. We must release our forgiveness.

When forgiveness is released, there is the peace of knowing that everything can be okay. Years ago I was reminded by the Lord not to keep a long list of wrongs others have done to me. It is easier to have a heartfelt apology and move on than it is to keep a list of wrongs. The Lord removed mine as far as the east is from the west, and I don't remember them anymore. Keeping a list of wrongs holds our hearts captive. It is easier to release our forgiveness than it is to carry it.

It is good to say what's in our hearts. I'm glad that I have a relationship like that with all my family members. It's a gift from God because family can be the hardest but most profitable ministry. They absolutely know who you are and see you at your weakest times. I try with all my heart not to keep the words that are sacred to me. This is why differences fade away and heartache leaves. I do miss the conversations that my mother-in-law and I had. I hold them close and dear to my heart. We have to cherish the time we have with each other because it is short. The conversations will be treasures to us. We won't be able to put a price on them.

When my mother-in-law found out the cancer was back, we all took a step back. She had lost a lot of weight, and getting around caused her pain. She never gave up her position that she would be healed, so we prayed. A few weeks before she passed, she went into the hospital. The doctors gave up hope and sent her home. Now we all had to stand together and seek the Lord. In my time with the Lord, he spoke again. He said, "I will receive her. The time is near."

My prayers were for mercy. I desired for her to have his mercy and peace. I wanted the Lord to spare her for our family. By this time it was almost three years since God had spoken about her. My heart was crying out for her. The night before Sharon died, my wife asked me the hardest question I have answered up until now. She asked, "What do you see and hear from God right now?"

I responded to her question hesitantly, but the Spirit rose up inside me and gave me the grace to answer. I knew it would be the answer she did not want to hear. One thing I knew for sure—I wanted to be there for her because I didn't want her to experience that loss. In these moments we know we truly are one as man and wife. We feel what our partners feel because we love them so much. I know I am not to carry anything with me. In Christ, our load is light and easy, but this troubled me to see her this way. I answered her, "She will be greatly received soon."

My wife began to weep, and she fell into my arms. I embraced her the best I knew how. It was hard to even rest that night. There were many things going on in my head, but all I knew to do was speak God's Word and pray. I cried out, "Thou Son of David, have mercy on her."

Many times I asked God for his mercy. I believe that he never failed to answer that prayer. I believe he answered me the first time I asked him. We woke up the next morning and went right back to Sharon's home to be with family. We spent all day there. Late in the evening my wife and I were both very tired. She needed to get out for a breath of fresh air, so she stepped out for a moment. She wanted to get the kids out of the house. She asked, "Will you sit with my mother?"

I replied, "Yes, I will."

I sat in the chair next to her and bowed my head to pray. I asked once more, "Thou Son of David, have mercy." The room was filled with presence of God. I could see the angels praying as well, and the great cloud of witness that was before us. Then, suddenly, I didn't see anything, but I knew he was there. His presence draws our hearts to the humblest place. My heart awaited his answer as it panted for him.

He answered so sweetly, "Look up. Your redemption is drawn near."

As I lifted my eyes, I saw him standing there by my mother-in-law. He grabbed her by the hand. He stooped down to her and looked at her, face to face. He spoke, "I come myself for my own."

Tears were streaming down my face. I was awed at what I saw. He put his hand on her face gently and caressed her. He then took in breath, and I could see the cancer leaving her body. He took it from her. Then he asked, "Sharon, are you ready?"

She replied, "Yes, Lord, I am." He took her by the hand and drew her to himself. It was the most beautiful exchange. His garments were spread out over her; it seemed as if he and she became one together. She was created in his likeness and image. I will always see this revelation as true. We are to become what we behold. We spend just brief moments in this life beholding the beauty of his Word. Then in a moment, in a twinkling of an eye, we are transformed into this beauty.

My mother-in-law and my wife and kids will always have the strongest bond. She waited for them to leave before she passed.

I believe this was God's way of protecting them. For me it was a great honor to be there with her as she had been there for us. We all still have our struggles, but I believe God allowed me to see in order to give us hope—a living and breathing hope.

CHAPTER TWELVE

◆

When Two Become One

In every moment of this act of love and mercy we can see the revealing of God and his nature toward creation. We can also see the blueprint of how he redeems us and reconciles us as one with himself. He truly turns the creature into a creation that carries the image of a living God. It is not anything that we earn by merit, but it is a gift from God. Jesus was a carpenter by trade in the earthly realm. In the spiritual realm he was also a carpenter, building and becoming the Word we need to overcome all we face in the earth.

His plan is for us to be emptied so he can fill us with something better. That something better is the Word of God. We are partakers of the flesh when we are born into this world, but when we are born again we are born into him and are an available vessel waiting to be used. He gave all of himself, and his fullness to humankind, so we must be emptied to receive. From the time Jesus entered the world, he reflected the goodness of the Father and did nothing on his own accord. He does only what the Father does because he was born of him for that purpose. He is the incarnate Word.

Jesus's purpose for us is to be so full of him that we don't look back on the world and its ways. He never took my life away; rather, he showed me a better way to live it. He replaced the nature I was born into. We are in the world but not of it. By design, we are supposed to return to him. He breathed and made us from that very breath and Word. To walk and be with God the way Adam was before the fall, we must return to that pure state. For this reason alone, the Word of God is an absolute necessity. It crucifies the flesh and reveals the true nature inside.

> I have been crucified with Christ. It is no longer I
> that live, but Christ who lives in me. And the life
> I know live in the flesh I live by faith in the Son
> of God, who loved me and gave himself to me.
> (Galatians 2:20)

My grandmother loved roses. My mother would buy her roses for every special occasion. When I was a kid I would visit her and even stay during the summer for a week. She took great care of her roses. Everyone could tell Grandma cherished the gift of the roses. They brought enjoyment to her life. There is much work involved when it comes to roses. They must be planted in the right soil, have plenty of sunshine, food, and water, and the dead flowers must be removed.

During the summertime the roses would be in full bloom, and Grandma would water them, especially saturating the ground so the moisture would reach the roots. The roots are the life of a plant. The blooms would start out closed, but as the sun shone on them, the blooms would open to display their beauty. We are the same way when it comes to the Word of God. He plants us, gives us plenty of sunshine and water, and he prunes the dead stuff from us so we can bear even more fruit in the seasons to come.

In the fall Grandma would prune the roses and prepare them for winter. As the season got colder, the rose petals would fall to the ground one by one until the bush was bare and had nothing but thorns. We often want to resemble the beauty of the rose when it is in full bloom, but there is a time of thorns in our lives. I believe God already has supplied all we need in any season. He wants us just to understand the leading he places on our hearts; only then he is opened to us.

When Jesus walked in his ministry on earth, he was in full bloom of the glory of God. He walked and talked with people. He healed and delivered them. He loved them and had mercy upon them. He fully demonstrated the actions of the Word of God. He was fully wrapped in flesh but knew no sin. He was opened to them in the full bloom of revelation. But like a rose in full bloom, the petals fell off as it became cold. Then all that was left was the thorns.

And being in agony He prayed more earnestly and His sweat became like drops of blood falling to the ground. (Luke 22:44)

Jesus was forced to wear these thorns upon his head as a crown. Before this happened He prayed in the garden until big drops of blood began falling to the ground. To live among the thorns is to live in a place of agony. It was a place of agony for Jesus too. As he interceded for humankind, his connection with the earthly realm became more apparent. We always want to return back to a garden, but it is in the tree that we find life. I could only imagine the droplets of blood falling from his forehead to the dirt. He was sealing the place of agony that took place in the garden. In Adam, we feel disconnected in the relationship, but in Christ we are made fully alive in it.

Jesus received the crown of thorns to relieve us from feeling disconnected and distant. He took Adam's curse of the thistles and thorns. When I think of how they buried those thorns deeply into his head, I know he would have done anything to shorten the gap between himself and his creation. There is no distance between us and God other than ourselves.

In him, the rose is always in full bloom and arrayed with his

119

glory. I know deep down inside that, without him, I would be thorns and thistles—a product of my own work. He is the dew that glistens on my petals. I am an example of craftsmanship built from his blueprint and plan, a rose planted in his presence. Just as I look upon my wife as a rose, he does the same. He loves all of it—the roots, the bloom, and the thorns.

> When the soldiers had crucified Jesus, they took his garments and divided them into four parts, one part for each soldier; also his tunic. But the tunic was seamless, woven in one piece from top to bottom. So they said to one another, "Let us not tear it, but cast lots for it to see whose it shall be." (John 19:23–24)

His tunic was seamless and woven in one piece from top to bottom. He even demonstrated that as he was among the people. It is a powerful visual to see his Word demonstrated. His desire is to encourage our hearts and knit them together in love. In love, we reach all the riches of full assurance of understanding. We understand the mystery of God, which is Christ. He was one piece, seamless and woven from top to bottom. This is how I see his people in faith. I see them as one, undivided and in Christ. He is the thread that knits us all together. Above all I see love, and God is love!

> See my servant will act wisely. He will be raised and lifted up and highly exalted. Just as there were many who were appalled at him, his appearance was so disfigured beyond that of any human being and his form beyond human likeness. (Isaiah 52:13–14)

From the cross Jesus displayed great authority and power. The image that he bore for you and me is the very sin we struggle with. He took the old nature upon himself. His appearance was so disfigured. He bore this image for all of humankind. Everything was placed upon his shoulders. His hands pierced and arms outstretched. He was holding up all the weight of the world upon himself.

He was raised in the place of the skull. He was lifted up and highly exalted above the place of death. When we know life, death cannot stop us. It cannot separate us from love. God is love, and we know him through the sacrifice of Jesus, his incarnate Word. He will lift us high above that place of death in our lives.

He declared, "It is finished!" (John 19:30)

The power was coming down as a sent word from God, and it was returning, lifted and highly exalted. With every demonstration from the cross Jesus was proved and witnessed. He had been sent, he had accomplished, and then he returned to his resting place at the right hand of the Father. His work was, is, and will be complete always and forever. He became the ladder for all humankind to use in order to cross the chasm of death into life.

He bowed his head and gave up the ghost. He was truly the mercy seat before the people. When we look into his mercy, we see God. We see him through the Word of God and his demonstrations of unfailing love. It is in the story of his death that we find eternal life with God. It is in this sacrifice that we find freedom. It is here that we see creature turned into the loving likeness and image.

My man in the mirror is gone! The stained glass has been washed over by the warm flow of his blood. The past is reconciled and set apart under the banner of his Word. The portrait I portrayed was, is, and always will be swallowed up by life itself. Death is defeated in the atmosphere of life himself. He, the Word made flesh, became what he loved so that we could become what he made us to be…the word in the earth. He allows us to let go and live!

Made in the USA
Middletown, DE
27 December 2017